# And Then Mark Died

To Carol —
With deep appreciation
for your commitment to
justice and service

May God continue
to work in and
through your life with grace
and power.

Fondly,
Susan

# And Then Mark Died

## Letters of Grief, Love, & Faith

Susan Sonnenday Vogel

Abingdon Press
*Nashville*

*For Mark*

# Contents

## The Letters

Grace to you and peace. Praise be to the God…whose consolation never fails us! [Who] comforts us in all our troubles, so that we in turn may be able to comfort others in any trouble of theirs and to share with them the consolation we ourselves receive from God.

—A letter from Paul

*My life was good, filled with grace and peace. We were ordinary people. We were people of faith, firm in what we believed, attempting to live in ways that made grace and peace real in the church and in the world.*

*And then Mark died.*

*Our twenty-three-year-old son was killed in an automobile accident.*

*Our world changed forever.*

# Our World Changed Forever

I did not know *then* what changes there would be and what they would mean. I learned, and I am still learning. Everyone around me is learning. Each of us learns and changes in a distinctive—and often surprising—way.

Among people of faith, there is a long tradition of writing letters about what is urgent and life changing. The apostle Paul wrote letters to those first fledgling communities. He wrote of his suffering and his hope, his grief over failure, his assurance of mercy, his proclamation of grace and promise of peace. Each letter had a distinctive character, for it brought a word crafted for a particular people.

I write to you out of the legacy of those communities. Shaped by the life and liturgies of the church, my suffering knows hope; my failure, mercy. I live in the assurance of grace and the promise that, in time, I will know peace.

I write to you and to others who have touched my life in particular ways, those from whom I have learned and those who have learned from our grief. I write to you and others through whom I know the consolation that never fails, so that I, in turn, may be able to comfort others in any trouble of theirs.

I want to tell you the truth, or at least my truth—the truth of grief, of love, of faith.

Two women for whom I have immense regard have given me pause. Through a character in her novel *The Blind Assassin*, Margaret Atwood cautioned, "The only way you can write the truth is to assume that what you set down will never be read." Anna Quindlan insisted she would never write a memoir. Originally a reporter, she feared—no, she knew—that she could not recall all the facts accurately: "Memory is such a shapeshifter of a thing. . . ."

I want to tell you the truth. I want you to read it, and I am not sure I recall all the facts accurately. At best, grief blurs. It distorts and obliterates.

Paul wrote what had been given to him. His sources, he said, were trustworthy. I write to you what has been given to me—shaped in the crucible of grief and refined with hope and grace. I write the truth I know. To some has been given other truth. This is mine, mingled with the cries and despair, the hopes and new life, of those who have blessed me with their truth.

Mark died on December 16, 1990, after having sustained critical injuries in an automobile accident on December 9th. Christmas that year brought hope and promise as never before. We know what it means to be carried by the love and prayers of the community of faith. We are terribly sad. We are also thankful.

We miss Mark. Our lives will never be the same. And we give thanks for the wonderful and turbulent, frustrating and awe-filled and good twenty-three years we had together. We know now that he is safe.

Mark had moved to Redlands, California, to start a new job. From Boston, he had driven across the country by himself and found it to be an exhilarating and challenging adventure. We are grateful he stopped to visit his brother David, grandparents, parents, and more family and friends. He called intermittently to describe the wonders of mountains, deserts, and all that was in between.

On December 9th he was returning home from a short trip and, trying to avoid slow-moving traffic after coming over a hill, lost control of the car. We were thankful, as he would have been, that no one else was injured.

Mark did not regain consciousness. We believe he knew, in some way, that we were there with him during the week before he died. Following Mark's death, we made his body available for organ donations. We are hopeful others have new life.

The memorial service for Mark was one of thanksgiving and redemption. We sang Easter hymns and prayed from our hymnal the service of death and resurrection. A week later we celebrated Christmas. And then we discovered, and continue to discover, what it means to go on with our lives.

Mark's younger brother, David, returned to the small town where he had his first job as a newspaper reporter. It was not long until, dissatisfied with his work, he moved to Boston and then applied to law school. He understood in his heart what some lightly say: "Life is too short. . . ." Life is, indeed, too short for him not to pursue work he loves.

Dick, who is Mark's father, and Tracy, Mark's step-mother, returned to their home and work in Kansas City, Missouri. Besides living into the reality of their own grief, they struggled to help their ten-year-old daughter, Emily, understand what it meant that her big brother Mark was dead.

My husband, Stuart, returned to reStart, his ministry in downtown Kansas City with persons who are homeless. In addition to facing the loss of a stepson he loved as a son, he has cared tenderly for me through these years of healing.

I returned to colleagues at Saint Paul School of Theology, many of whom understood, thankfully, that I was not going to "be better" very soon. Five years after Mark's death, I was ready to put words to my own grief and first intimations of healing. Over several more years, I created these letters in an effort to recompose my own world and speak to sisters and brothers of faith.

I want to tell you the truth. I want you to read it. I hope you will never forget. I pray you will come to know anew the One whose consolation never fails us, and be able to comfort others in any trouble of theirs.

Grace to you and, in time, peace.

*Susan*

# To My Wise Teacher

## Dear Bob,

Thank you and Ann for your thoughtful words. How curious that Mark and your mother died the same day. I know how you have grieved her dying over many years as she slipped away from being the woman she had been. And during our weeklong vigil at the hospital, I think we knew—we surely feared—that Mark was no longer the remarkable young man he had been.

As I try to make sense of our loss, and wander about in grief and confusion, I have been thinking about all I learned as I studied with you. You taught me more than you could imagine. I have tried many times to find the right words to tell you.

You go to college to learn from one great teacher, someone said. I thought of you. I did not know forty years ago that that was what I was doing when I arrived at DePauw. I did learn from others, but nothing comes close to the learning that grew from the work I did with you.

You taught me to be a careful theologian. Week upon week, as I wrote concise papers on Christian doctrine, you made me see how one tiny shift can have monumental implications in one's faith. The nature of Christ: God or like God? *Homo-ousia* or *homoi-ousia*? The same substance or not quite the same?

We worked with painstaking care to distinguish between immortality and resurrection. "Immortality" is Greek, not Hebrew, you said, and is not the primary understanding in the Christian tradition. "Eternal life," in New Testament terms, does not have to do with life after death. It is the life lived in Christ—starting right now and continuing forever. We talked about Greek and Hebrew understandings of body/soul. The Bible rarely understands a soul apart from its bodily life. So, at death, we die—our whole self dies. And our whole self awaits resurrection. It was always so clear.

And then Mark died.

A friend gave me a quote from Roger Kahn that begins, "The world is never again as it was before anyone you love has ever died; never so innocent, never so fixed, never so gentle, never so pliant to your will. . . ." I wonder if it could be paraphrased to say, "The world of one's theology is never again as it was. . . ."

It is not so fixed, so pliant to the logic I have always brought to it. I dream about Mark. I hear him telling me to move on with my life. I sometimes have a sense of his presence that does not fit with the finality of death until that day of resurrection. And the strange thing (strange for me, who always has had to figure things out and have *the* answer) is that I do not have to understand or try to explain how or where or when.

What has become important to me is, simply, the word of Paul.

"If we live, we live to the Lord, and if we die, we die to the Lord; so then, whether we live or whether we die, we are the Lord's."

For right now, I give thanks for the assurance that Mark is held in God's love, and that nothing in all creation can separate any of us from the love of God we know in Christ Jesus. I do not need to explain the in-between times. I do not need to figure out "where" he is. I do not understand about God's time and our time. But that does not mean that "resurrection" is unimportant.

*The resurrection of the body and the life everlasting.*

I learned the Creed in confirmation class and have said it most Sundays for more than forty years. The Sunday after Mark died we returned to worship. I expected I would cry through the music and prayers. I was not prepared for what happened to my voice as we said those familiar words. Tears came and my voice caught as I affirmed, "I believe in the resurrection of the body and the life everlasting."

It used to be "a doctrine of the church." I wrote papers about it, and when I was preparing to be ordained, I had to define what I understood it to mean. Somehow I do not remember much of what I thought was important about those words through all of that explaining.

Now it has to do with the everlasting life of my son, the resurrection of this body to which I first gave birth. It is not now an esoteric exercise in creedal affirmation. It is my fervent mother-hope that my baby, my firstborn child, is not lost forever, is not lost *to me* forever, is not lost.

I used to be amused at questions about what our bodies would be like in the resurrection—whether we would recognize one another. What did it matter? It matters now.

In one sense, I feel foolish asking the questions. Apparently, though, people have been asking them since the beginning of question-asking. And judging from Paul's extensive responses, it was a lively issue in the churches at Rome and Corinth. I do not need an answer, which is a good thing since I am not likely to find a definitive one. I do need "pieces" to put together that are more than simply a doctrine. I need to have a grounding for my living without Mark in this life—and what it means for me to affirm the resurrection of *his* body and *his* everlasting life.

I was surprised by how helpful it was when I read these words from H. Richard Niebuhr: "I do not believe that death has been conquered because I know that Christ rose from the dead. I believe that Christ rose from the dead, because I know that death has been conquered."

Aidan Kavanagh, writing in the Yale Divinity School journal *Reflections*, says this "thought itself seems worth rescuing from those who are merely literate in theology." As he understands what Niebuhr is saying, "the resurrection of Jesus the Christ is not so much the first cause of death's conquest but a symptom of it." A deep truth throughout Hebrew and Christian scripture is that "the whole saving history of God's dealings with [God's people] is a tale of the steady overcoming of death and its dominion in our lives." God in Christ comes bringing life. Christians begin life by dying to all that is past in baptism, "after which they never die again."

I am not sure I know what that looks like. Perhaps I am back to the assurance that Mark lives in God's love, as he always has. In God's wisdom, we will know resurrection in the way God has planned for us. I can go on with Niebuhr and say that, because I know death has been conquered, I know that there is resurrection.

In one sense, I know already that resurrection is true. For, in a way that may be an intimation of what is to come, I have been brought to new life out of the agony of death and loss. With Mark's death, I knew death. And God has brought me out of that death into a life that has the miracle of new strength. An intimation.

Nietzsche, whom I do not have many occasions to quote, wrote, "What fails to kill me only makes me stronger." That is, indeed, a resurrection I have known. I know of others who have been killed by their loss—become ill, are broken in spirit, give up, stop living—though they may continue to survive.

A most powerfully poignant statement of deepened and

strengthened life comes from an Iranian churchman whose son had been murdered.

O God
Our son's blood has multiplied the fruit of the Spirit in the soil of our souls;
So when his murderers stand before thee on the day of judgement
Remember the fruit of the Spirit by which they have enriched our lives.
And forgive.

—Bishop Denqani-Tafti

It is hard to fathom how one could move to that depth of forgiveness, but I keep reading it and trying to understand. What I *do* understand is that God has multiplied the fruits of the Spirit in the soil of my soul and has created life all over again. An intimation of resurrection.

God continues to work in and through me—and in all of us touched by Mark in his living and dying—to bring healing through the cutting away of all that would threaten us, and bring new life and strength and growth. Is that to misunderstand, or even trivialize, resurrection?

I do not know how it will be in the end time. I live in the promise that God, in God's own wisdom, will keep us in love and grace, and that we will know a new heaven and a new earth. In the between time, I know that God has brought me "a mighty long way," has made a way for life when all I knew was death, and has set me on a path to witness to others who know only death. An intimation, a foretaste.

*I believe in the resurrection of the dead and the life everlasting. Amen.*

My thanks,

*Susan*

# To Our Pastor

## Dear Emanuel,

During these past six years, I do not know how I would have lived without the ministry of St. James. Whenever Pat begins to sing, "Through it all, God brought me through, . . ." I give thanks for you and for the congregation. I believe God has worked in and through you and this extraordinary community of faith to bring us new life and hope for the future.

It began with your sermon the day of Mark's accident. It was compelling and poignant at the time, before we knew what was ahead. It took on a meaning I never could have foreseen as we lived the agony of the next week.

One phrase lived with me: "Hope was the last thing in Pandora's box." Hope. How I grasped on to that word. And, yet, it was sometimes hard to know what it was for which we were hoping. At first we hoped to get to the hospital and discover that Mark would be all right. Then, as the week wore on, and on, our hope grew more confused.

All assurances were gone. All that had been certain in our lives was being peeled away. The last thing in the box, all that we had, was hope. As I sat in the tiny hospital chapel and prayed my confused prayer, I kept hearing your words.

Hope. Who hopes for what she can see? Our hope changed. Perhaps what happened is that we discovered hope. It was "wishing" that we had been doing, wishing for a particular thing—for Mark to wake up and still be Mark. When we feared that was not going to happen, we no longer knew what to want. Out there were so many unknowns, so many alternatives, so many unimaginable consequences to whatever happened. We no longer knew what to want.

That is when I ceased wanting and wishing, and began to hope. Perhaps that is what is meant by hope being the very last thing in the box. Hope moved the outcome—as it always, of course, had been—out of my hands, out of my wishing and wanting. But now I *knew* that it did not depend upon what I wanted and wished. I became hopeful, and my hope did not have a particular object. I hoped and prayed that God would continue to hold and protect Mark. I prayed that, if he could not be better, he would not survive. I did not know what I meant by "better." I bargained with God about how I would arrange my life to care for him, no matter what.

It was hope that sustained me in those hours and days. It was the trust and conviction that God does work in all things for good, and would work in and through this tragedy of ours to bring healing. I hoped for healing, and I no longer knew what healing would look like.

My hope was not betrayed. Healing came for Mark in his dying, for healing was no longer possible in what we call living.

Hope continues. Healing continues. I live in the hope that his dying is not the end. I live in the hope that God is bringing redemption, for Mark and for us, in and through all that happened. I live in hope.

Recently I read words by Sister Joan Chittister that describe the hope I know.

Hope . . . takes life on its own terms, knows that whatever happens God lives in it. . . . Despair says that there is no place to go but here. . . . Hope sends us dancing around dark corners trusting in a tomorrow we cannot see.

The problem is that we always think of hope as grounded in the future. Wrong. Hope is always grounded in the past. Hope simply challenges us to remember, always, that we have survived everything in life to this point.

The old song we sing is about grace, but this stanza says all that any of us could sing about hope:

Through many dangers, toils, and snares, I have already come; 'tis grace hath brought me safe thus far, and grace will lead me home.

Some time after Mark died, during a particularly rough time, an image you used in another sermon brought me hope anew. Do you remember when you talked about sheep that are caught in a storm? When a storm comes up in the cold of winter, and the wind comes from behind the sheep and blows the icy rain under their wool, they will freeze to death. As the storm comes, the sheep must turn to face into the storm. I do not suppose they choose to do that. You said that sheep are not very bright and must be carefully guided by the sheepdogs and shepherd. It is the shepherd and dogs that turn the sheep to face into the storm so that they will survive.

I saw then that that was what God was doing for me— turning me to face the storm, and staying with me so that I could live. What a marvelous image. What hope it brought in the hardest of days.

Through the years, I have watched and listened as others moved into grief and then began healing. I observed that having a very hard time is often a sign that healing is happening. At first, the numbness and denial are so pervasive that the pain can hardly be experienced. But as we grow stronger and more aware of what is happening, more pain can be taken in. It gets worse before it gets better, they say. Were the numbness to continue, we would slowly die, frozen to death by the icy rain. But God has turned me toward the storm so I will live.

Your presence and wisdom through these days and months and years of healing have been a blessing, and I think it is largely because you have known sorrow and have witnessed to the way in which God has worked through your own tragedies to bring new life.

I thought about you when I read portions of a sermon Gardner Taylor preached to a group of "brothers in ministry."

> "And my brother preachers, you say that you want great power to move among [people's] heartstrings? You cannot have that without great sorrow. [God] can fill only the places that have been emptied of the joys of this life. . . ."

> "Now you may tickle people's fancies, but you will never preach to their hearts, until at some place, some solemn appointment has fallen upon your own life, and you have wept bitter tears, and gone to your own Gethsemane and climbed your own Calvary. That's where power is!"

Taylor concludes his sermon by saying what he understands to be the power of proclamation:

> "It is not in the tone of the voice. It is not in the eloquence of the preacher. It is not in the gracefulness of [the] gestures. It is not in the magnificence of [the] congregation. It is in a heart broken, and put together, by the eternal God!"

Emanuel, you have preached to our hearts and have brought strength. May God continue to do that remarkable work in and through you.

Our love and prayers,

*Susan*

# To Witnesses in Song

## Dear Pat,

Your care and your words of comfort have been gifts to me. I treasure the way you ask how I am—with a look that knows that the joy that comes with the morning only comes after many nights of weeping. I did not understand how you could know until I heard you sing.

Each time the familiar melody begins and you step forward, I anticipate my tears. You touch a place deep within my sorrow.

> Somehow I made it—
>   Somehow I made it—
> Through it all, God brought me through.

The way in which you have paraphrased that song is a particular blessing for me now: "Somehow I am making it. . . ." Someday, in God's own time, we may be able to sing, "I made it. We made it." That is the hope and the promise. It is important to be able to affirm, as you beautifully do, that—in the meantime—we *are* making it, in God's power.

There have been those Sundays when you have stopped in the midst of the song and, with the choir continuing behind you, shared your testimony about the hard time you had just come through. The words became, then, not simply the songwriter's words. They were your own—and have become all of ours.

Do you remember the night of the reStart dinner when Daybreak sang? As you were closing, Michael began to play the familiar melody. It was there that I first heard you sing,

Somehow *we* made it, somehow *we are making it*.
Through it all God brought us through.

It was clear anew that we do not "make it" as solitary, lonely individuals, with God taking each of us by the hand. God counts on us to take one another by the hand and move together through hard times. It is through the community of faith, through sisters and brothers, that God brings us through.

I looked around the room that night and saw Cheryl, who had once been homeless, and now was serving others who needed a safe and warm place of hospitality. I saw Helen, who had been among the first volunteers and had coordinated hundreds of others, and now found reStart to be her home. One remarkable young family was beginning life anew in a home they would soon own. And all around were those who wanted to be a part of this ministry of hospitality, for—in ways no one else may have known—each of us knew that somehow God was bringing us through.

Those words, and your witness as you sing them, have become my hope, my strength. You sing in the community of those who have faced hardship and suffering and what looks like defeat, whether it is on Sunday morning at St. James or at the reStart dinner. And I gain strength in the knowledge that you and so many others are making it. How many in our congregation have lost a child? How many are suffering grief each day? I am not alone in my sorrow. When I can look at other bereaved parents like Royce and Barbara and Don, and see the joy and strength that they know, I can make it for another week. God, with the witness and prayers of so many, is bringing us through.

When a young person who has been spared much pain in her life sings of living through the storms, one can simply be thankful that she has a powerful faith in her precious Lord and rejoice in her good life. But when someone like you sings from your pain and sorrow and, out of that storm, witnesses to the all-powerful hand of God bringing you through, then you bring hope and promise to all of us who fear we are drowning. You may never know the ways your witness has helped us find a way where there was no way.

Thank you for letting me see your own sorrow. It makes your faith-filled confidence mean everything to me. Trust always that you are in my prayers. May God surround you each day with the hope and promise to which you witness.

*Susan*

## Dear Royce,

Whenever I think of you, I envision you as you stepped to the front of the choir on a Sunday morning. The chords were familiar, the music rhythmic and upbeat. You began to sing, with almost a grin.

> I can depend on God, I can depend on God,
> through the storm, through the rain,
> through the sickness, through the pain,
> I can depend, I can depend, I can depend on God.

You sang with enthusiasm, "full of spirit." We enjoyed the beat, the stirring words, that look you had.

Then our world changed. Mark died. The next Sunday, when you sang that song, we heard it again, for the first time.

> Through the storm . . .
> Through the pain . . .
> I can depend . . . on God.

> I was lost, couldn't find my way.
> Stayed with me each and every day.
> I was sick, couldn't get well,
> Healed my body, I can tell,
> I can depend, I can depend, I can depend on God.

Through the words came a moment of comfort, tears to wash away a piece of the agony, the promise that God does not go away.

Two years passed. Each time you sang I felt a bit more strength, and I could begin to believe the rumor that healing might be possible.

One Sunday I read in the bulletin that your mother had died. As you sang, I could hear your own pain and loss. And then, it was just three months later you heard those awful words: Your young son is dead. I ached with you, prayed for you, cried for your grief and mine.

It seemed so soon. I heard those familiar chords, looked up, and you were moving to the front of the choir. How could you do it?

> . . . through the storm, through the rain
> through the sickness, through the pain,
> . . . I can depend on God.

And I heard it again, as if for the first time.

What does it take to sing before the congregation two weeks after you have buried your dear fifteen-year-old? What does it take? A faith that knows "through the storm and sickness and pain, I can depend on God."

No longer was it an anthem. It was witness. It was witness to the faithfulness of God who "stays with me each and every day."

You know I continue to pray for you. You know how mightily your witness strengthens me each time I hear you. You bring me hope and promise and assurance. And I will keep sending to you words I have discovered that may bring healing for you as they do for me. With you, I am coming to understand what Paul meant when he wrote to the church at Rome.

> I want to bring you some spiritual gift to make you strong; or rather, I want to be among you to be myself encouraged by your faith as well as you by mine.

What a mystery. How can I, in my grief, be sustained by you, while you, in your need, look to me and other hurting sisters and brothers for help? From where does the strength come?

I think Paul knew. As he wrote to the churches at Rome and Corinth, he was clear about God's strength and power and wisdom working in our weakness—especially in our weakness. We are the vessels of clay, the pots of earthenware, that contain the treasure. This proves that such transcendent power does not come from us, but is God's alone.

A mystery. A mystery by which grieving and hopeless sisters and brothers are carried by one another through the power of our God and into hope.

We are stewards of the mysteries of God, Paul wrote. And so it seems that once I have known this sustaining power through you, and you through me, I am called to be a faithful steward of that mystery. It is as if I cannot but live that witness. The stewardship of that witness has been handed over to me, and to you—a treasure that we dare not bury.

Thank you, my dear friend. Thank you. You have sung

me into the mystery. My soul is filled. My body knows healing.

I can depend, I can depend, I can depend on God.

*Susan*

## *Dear Mary K.,*

During those very hard years while you were working for the city, I often picked up the morning paper and wondered how you could do it: the stinging words of those who opposed you, the lack of money to care for those who needed special help, the picky complaints. Then on Sunday morning I watched you sing.

You sang of your many burdens. But you sang also of the trust you had in the One who could carry them all. You had, as some say, turned it all over. As you stood straight and assured among the choir, I knew that you were telling me how you got through each day.

When your mother became ill, and you had to make hard decisions about her care, I wondered how you could do that, on top of everything else. And then I saw you singing on Sunday morning.

Again, I knew you were turning it over to the One you trusted, our God who would carry it for you.

When Mark died, some said that they wondered if I could allow anyone to take care of me. I always had been strong, self-sufficient. At least, that was how it seemed to other people.

The phone call came. Mark had been critically injured. Suddenly I was no longer able to maintain a semblance of self-sufficiency and strength. I tried at first. I had to. My whole world was off balance, and I had to hold on to some order. I kept needing to take care of things—pack a bag, make plane reservations, cancel a lunch appointment, figure out what had to be covered at work.

Finally Stuart insisted on fixing the soup. A friend called to say not to worry about the appointments for the week. I left for Las Vegas to stand by Mark's bed and be completely helpless.

Whenever something had happened before to someone I loved, I worked to make things better. Sometimes I succeeded. Often, not. But I tried. I did not know how to do otherwise. I had to do *something*.

And now, in the most critical time I had ever faced, I came to know there was nothing I could do. I could do nothing to make Mark better. I could not even care for myself and carry out my responsibilities. A note I wrote in my improvised diary, after making a call back to school, said simply, "I have now let go of that. Others will have to do it."

Some wondered if I could let others care for me and take over my work. I had come to the end of my strength. I had no choice. I turned it all over. I put it all in God's hands and in the hands of those whom God provided.

Apart from this kind of tragedy, would I have ever learned how insufficient I am all by myself? All of my burdens and problems have always been in God's hands. I had never carried these burdens alone. Now I know it.

I forget sometimes. I think I have to do it all, carry every burden. But I have known the end of the myth of self-sufficiency, as I know you have. When I forget, I see you in my mind, singing confidently.

I see you singing about your burdens and singing also of the One who carries them. And I am reminded afresh that God will do "abundantly far more than all we can ask or imagine." Into God's hands I can put all that I am and each burden I bear—where you know they always have been.

My prayers,

*Susan*

# To My Husband

Valentine's Day

## My dearest Stuart,

Today seems the right day to write a letter to you about you and me and how we lived through Mark's death and have survived these last five years.

I know that I love you more today than I have ever loved you, and I know that you now love me too, in ways we never knew were possible when we made vows to keep a covenant that was "becoming."

Some are pulled apart and destroyed by the loss we have known. So we might say that we have grown in our love and commitment in spite of Mark's death. It may be more true to talk of what has happened in the face of his dying— not in spite of it or because of it, but never apart from what it has meant for both of us.

I remember that first dreadful night. We returned from seeing the Nutcracker Ballet. Dick called about the accident. It was bad, he said. We had no idea then how bad it was—or was going to be. You held me.

It was hard for us to plan together what to do next. I needed to keep doing things for myself, and the only way you knew to care for me was to do those things for me. Finally you fixed soup so I would eat. It gave us both something to do.

There was not anything to say. We waited. We waited for more word about Mark. We waited until it was time to go to the airport. We waited. And then as you put Dick and Tracy and me on the plane, neither of us knew what to say. "I love you." It was enough.

Through the agonizing week of vigil at the hospital, I ached for the moments I could stand by Mark's bed and watch him, talk to him, wonder if he could hear, ponder if he was Mark anymore. Then I had to call you. I needed to hear you and tell you what was happening, even when nothing was happening. Especially when nothing was happening.

You seemed so far away. You tried to be close. You were alone and had your own grieving. Perhaps you knew, or allowed yourself to know, sooner than I, that Mark was not going to survive, or would never truly recover. A part of me kept hoping, but I think you knew.

When I called to tell you, you seemed already to have accepted it. No, not acceptance. Would you ever accept it? You had already sensed it. You knew.

I came home. It is hard for me to imagine how you could decorate the Christmas tree that evening while you were waiting. I think it has been hard for you to decorate the tree ever since. But it was a blessed welcome, and a first sign that there was a future beyond the dreadful present.

We did not know how to help each other. You needed to go to work, to have a place to go, something to do. We got through those early days with all the people around. They left, and we were alone.

Evening after evening I crawled into your lap and cried. You went upstairs. I sat in the dark and cried more. You were so silent. I did not know how you were feeling, how you were grieving. It must have been hard for you to feel helpless. So we kept trying to do our work, and do our lives. There were hard times, and harder times. Then a few better days. We both must have decided that we were going to get on with our lives, though we never spoke the words.

There were a few milestones in those first two years. We did go to the Nutcracker the next Christmas, though not on the usual Sunday afternoon. And that marvelous surprise party you and David planned for me—the happiest day I had had since Mark died. Bittersweet, too.

Then it was November. Your heart surgery. I was so afraid, and sobbed with relief and thanksgiving when they said you would be all right. They had tried to prepare me for how terrible you would look. I thought you looked wonderful!

It all helped us begin to heal together. You felt better, and each time I heard you describe the nurse climbing up over you and pounding on your chest, I knew you were thankful to be alive in a way that only happens when you have been to the edge.

Having discovered anew how fragile and precious life is, we dared to begin to know joy again. When Mark died, we learned about that precious and fragile life, but I think we were too numb and broken to begin to live the good parts of that discovery.

Another year. Another November. Hank called. We saw him at the hospital. Then you were the one he asked to tell his parents that he had AIDS. A month later he was dead. A tragic loss of a gifted and winsome young friend. I remember how you slammed your hands against the steering wheel when we left the hospital. As you raged about Hank's illness and dying, you began to say how angry you were about Mark's death.

When you finally shouted, and whispered, your anger,

another kind of healing began for us. You talked about Mark often at the time of Hank's death. We finally talked together about Mark and all we had lost.

I wish you and Mark could have come to know, in a better way than either of you did, how much you cared for each other and appreciated and respected each other. It was hard for both of you to say and to show it. And to know it.

Though you have not ever said it, I think that you have since then tried to tell those you love how important they are to you. It has seemed that way with Hank and our David, and the other David—the one who was once homeless, for whom you became the only father he could love.

Today, as I sit in the Cambridge flat, in the midst of a magical time, I think of you out on a strange road in a strange car driving on the strange side of the road. I am thankful for every moment we have, and it is difficult for me not to worry about you. I always have. But I feel anew how joy has come into our lives, and how much I treasure our life together.

The grief is not over. Our healing is not complete. I do not expect that will ever happen. What is different is that we are in that healing together now.

I do not understand all the ways in which God works in and through our tragedies to bring new life. I only know that what has happened to us feels like a miracle. We were broken and unable to make it better. In the midst of our tragedy, our healing began. In the midst of more tragedy, new healing began. I do not understand. I simply pray for you, and for us, every morning, and give thanks every night for our life. And for years to come.

I love you. I love you.

*S.*

March 30. Two years later.

Here we are again in the midst of grief upon grief. So many losses in such a short time. I heard others ask how you could preach such powerful and poignant funeral sermons for your own brother and your sister-in-law—and make it through. You were quiet, but later you said it would be Dale's service that would be the tough one. Thirty years of friendship.

No one could make you laugh the way Dale did as you rehearsed stories of those years. You rejoiced in the good times and—after you had some distance—you could laugh about Dale's bizarre hallucinations when he had been drinking and the dozens of times you took him to "detox" and treatment. Finally, he was truly recovering, but it was too late for his body to heal.

I had a strange reaction as I watched you suffer with planning what you were going to say at his memorial service. I felt angry at Dale for asking you to do that. You were the one who loved him longest, and, next to Joyce and his children, most. How could he expect you to do that, in the midst of your own grief? Why could you not be ministered unto at this time?

Then I remembered how much Dale loved you—closer than any brother, he said. And how intimately he knew you—how you are and what you need. He knew that you had to *do* something. You had to do something for him, a last thing for him. In the midst of your grieving, what you always need is to *do* something.

And so Dale gave you this gift, the opportunity to do one more thing for him. I have trouble saying he "would have" loved it. Somehow, he *did* love it and, as he promised, is whispering in God's ear good things about you.

And here we are, needing to grieve again. Is it possible to learn from times before? Or is each episode so different that we have to start all over?

It is good that there will be more to *do*. That is how it will need to be for a while. Joyce will need you. "Thank you for sharing your husband so much during these days," she said. She has others close to her, but you bring a special connection to Dale, and she needs you to stay close by.

What then? You have been grieving for a long time. We knew he was dying. But that is not the same.

Now he is gone. The banter is gone. You grieve the loss of that which you affectionately call palaver. The storytelling is gone. There are no more trips to plan together. No theology to argue. The faxes that captured all that wisdom from the Internet, along with outrageous cartoons, have stopped, and there will not be another of his masterful Christmas letters.

Gone also, thank God, are the suffering and the fear of life without dignity.

How do we go on unless we trust the promise and keep praying words of hope?

> Eternal God,
> For all that Dale has given us to make us what we are,
>     for that of him that lives and grows in each of us,
>     and for his life that in your love will never end,
>     we give you thanks. . . .
>
> Into your hands we commend your servant.
> We know that no mortal life you have made is without eternal meaning. No earthly fate is beyond your redeeming.
>
> Through your grace that can do far more than we can think or imagine, fulfill in Dale your purpose that reaches beyond time and death.

You have lost your best friend. But you will never lose what he has given you to make you what you are. You will always treasure that of him that lives and grows in you. And your faithfulness to what you carry with you is one way God fulfills Dale's purpose, beyond time and death.

And what do you still carry of Mark?

There is more you will do for Dale, for Mark, beyond time and death. You do it each day. You create second chances—and third, and seventy times seven chances. You live tough and passionate love. You do not give up. Beyond time and death, you love. Beyond time and death, Dale lives. Mark lives.

I love you.

*S.*

# To My Son David

## Dear David,

"Among the greatest delights parents can have is to see how their children love and enjoy each other."

When your Uncle John said those words in his "father toast" at Chris's wedding, I remembered. Your cousin Colin had just toasted Chris with his poignant words of a thankful younger brother and best friend.

I remembered you and Mark.

When we brought you home, Mark wrapped his arms around your tiny body. He hugged you and laughed. He was confused when you did not laugh with him but began to cry. Looking up with a quivering lip, he joined you with tears. He was not yet two, and your arrival had suddenly and radically changed his world. I fear he did not enjoy you much at first.

As you got a little older, you did enjoy each other. I look at the pictures and watch the Super 8 movies your dad took. You were very small and Mark was bent over, helping you stack the blocks and laughing with you as you knocked them over. You sat in your high chair, picked up a Cheerio, and gleefully stuffed it into Mark's mouth. You grew bigger and wrapped your arms around each other's shoulders as you grinned at the camera.

"Among the greatest delights parents can have is to see how their children love and enjoy each other."

As I recall that father toast, I think Uncle John added another word. "Among the greatest delights parents can have is to see how their *adult* children love and enjoy each other."

Adult children. Did you ever have a chance to love and enjoy each other as adult children? Something changed. Sometime, somewhere, as you and Mark entered your peculiar and frightening teens, your paths diverged. Your interests and values grew apart. You did not seem to enjoy each other. You loved each other. You simply did not know what to *do* with Mark, nor he, with you. Could you understand each other?

And then Mark died.

I grieve over your grief. I fear your grief has shadows of regret and ambivalence. Shadows of "what might have been" and "what if." Has it been more difficult to grieve, knowing the divergences between you and Mark?

You were clear even from those first terrible days after Mark died: Your life *would* go on. When everyone had left that December funeral day, and we were there alone—the family that now was our family—you set the course: "We *will* have Christmas."

You were right. All of our lives needed to go on. And we needed Christmas. We needed Christmas in ways we had never known we needed it. We needed the promise that there was still news of great joy—somewhere. It felt like a distant rumor.

Your life would go on. When you decided not to talk about Mark's death in your new office, or at law school, you were going on with your life, in the way you needed to do. Your brother was not defining you in his death. He had not in life.

Not long ago, you referred to the year after Mark died. The worst year of my life, you said. What did you do with all that was "worst"? How did you keep on? What did you become that was different? How has Mark's death changed you?

You had already taken on reliability and excellence. You had begun to look like the first child, and your differences seemed to pull you apart. Were there times of alienation? Do teenaged brothers ever escape alienation?

I grieve that you and Mark did not get another chance.

"Among the greatest delights parents can have is to see how their adult children love and enjoy each other."

I grieve that you and Mark never were adults together. You had brief times, but not long. Not long enough. You cannot grow as adults together.

Your Uncle John and Aunt Cathy and I struggled through the years. We had our hurts and demons that we feared sharing with one another. We made judgments without knowing one another's agony. We did not understand. We did not know how.

Then I discovered how wrong I was to make judgments when I had no sense of what my brother and sister were facing in their lives. My heart softened. Something new began.

Some of us get another chance. We get more time to find out "what if," to shorten the distance, to practice the enjoying.

That is why we looked forward to all of the family being together for Chris's wedding. It was as if we were a new family. We were coming in anticipation of a joy and love we had not celebrated before. For all of us to be together was a sign of healing we had not known.

Then we got there, and we remembered—we were not all there.

I have sometimes quoted a poet who says that "the deeper that sorrow carves into your being, the more joy you can contain." In the midst of the wedding, I knew also the truth that the more joy fills your heart, the more poignant the sorrow that accompanies it.

Some of us get another chance. You and Mark did not. I grieve your grief.

I have seen that you have found ways to go on and live your life. What I look for is the assurance that you are living *your* life. Some grief books talk about "the replacement child," one who is planned and conceived to replace one who has died. A surviving child can also become the replacement child. That has been my fear. It is my fear that you will believe that you must take Mark's place and your own as well. I fear that you will feel you have to make up for the loss by being more than you are.

When you decided to come back closer to home for law school, I was afraid you felt as if you had to. I was afraid you felt as if you had to be everything for me and for Stuart, for your dad and Tracy, for Emily.

That is why I have tried, always, to love you lightly. I want to love you lightly because I love you completely. I love *you*.

You are a rare mix of unfailing responsibility and engaging humor, persistence and tender regard for people, competence in all your work and the good sense not to do it all the time. I fear that the responsible and competent side will overtake the joyful parts of your world. I fear that the reliable part of you may feel you must make up for the ways in which Mark was not always as reliable as you, not always being here when we wished he were here—for his not being here, ever again.

I love you lightly.

I look at the demands upon your life, and I love you

lightly. I will not add to the demands upon you. I am afraid you will respond. I am afraid you will have to respond. Your reliability and your tender regard will make you. That is how you are.

I love you lightly. I love you for the irreplaceable, unique, precious adult child you are. I treasure you. I rejoice that you decided at the beginning that you would live your life.

I grieve that you and Mark did not have another chance. Who can know what might have been? I could not have imagined that my brother and sister and I would enjoy one another the way we did during the wedding weekend. I could not have imagined how often we would need one another and call to ask for care and support. I could not have imagined ending each call with "I love you." I know no other word to describe it all than *miracle*.

Your miracle was beginning: the miracle of brother-ness. You trekked across Boston so you two could party together. A friend wrote that Mark often talked about you and was so proud of your achievements. He even sat in the rain to celebrate your graduation. Then we laughed and loved and enjoyed around the table that graduation night as our family ate what would be our last meal together.

Who can know what might have been, at the hands of One who can do abundantly far more than we can ask or imagine?

I can see what *is*. You have taken your love for Mark into your life, and it is a good part of you. It is what keeps the responsible and competent side of you from overtaking the life-giving and tender parts. It is what reminds you what is important. In a vocation where all is serious, you do not take yourself too seriously.

In his life, in his death, Mark does not define you. In his life and his death, he has changed you. Your "no" to his death means you do go on with your life. And it is a life that will always announce: "We will have Christmas." For we know Easter.

I live in the assurance that you love Mark and forgive the hard times. I live in the trust that you know that you are treasured and irreplaceable. I live in love for you that is light and complete.

*Mom*

# To Mark's Father

## Dear Dick,

They used to call us a broken family. Now euphemisms take the place of that stark description. It is true, though. We are broken. We are not the family you and I planned.

In the first moments of young love, as you closed your hand around mine, this is not what we imagined. That Thanksgiving break when everyone else was snowbound, and you walked five miles to see me, this is not the family we dreamed. In the letters we wrote each day we were apart, this is not the family we described.

Something happened. Many somethings happened. Neither of us could understand all of it.

I am like the comic-strip character Cathy: "I am the product of two generations. . . . I'm juggling two generations of values, two generations of dreams, and two generations of guilt." I did not juggle well. My juggling was exceptionally poor during what some call the turbulent '60s. Unfortunately, that was when we were building the foundation of our marriage— on two generations of values and dreams. The fault lines were too great. It broke. I live with two generations of guilt.

You tried. I tried. We tried in different ways. It broke. A children's book popular in 1975 still said, "Boys build houses. Girls clean houses. Girls can cook. Boys eat what girls cook. Boys invent things. Girls use what boys invent." That was the year I was ordained. It was the year I went to work full-time. Two generations of values and dreams. It was the year we were divorced.

I did not juggle well. I made mistakes. I asked you one day, after it was "irretrievably broken," if you would forgive me. You said I did not need to ask that. I said I did. I believe you said yes: You did forgive me.

I went to a meeting wiping away tears that evening. A sometimes thoughtful, often judgmental, church lady said, "I thought you wanted this. I thought *you* wanted the divorce." I did. I did not juggle well. Still I grieve that it broke. We did not live happily ever after. It was not what we planned. Maybe there is not a happily ever after. I worry that I did not try hard enough—when our life was no longer happy. I have regrets.

I do have regrets, but they pale when I look at who and what we have become. I look at you and Tracy, the marriage you have created—so different from ours. Better, I believe. I see Emily, your daughter who would not have been. I watch how you have risked changing vocations. I fear I would have kept you from risking.

I would not be with Stuart. I may not have risked either without his "Why not?" He says that without me there would be a lot more homeless people on cold streets. Who can tell? I have regrets, but they are overtaken by gratitude for what is.

I see the kind of parents you and Tracy together have been for Mark and David and Emily. How I cherish how we have managed to be a family—how, as the boys were growing up, we created a stable place for them.

I have never been more thankful for the ways we are family than during those heart-crushing days of December as we hovered around Mark and watched him die. As awful as were those days, and many days since, I do not see how I could have borne them without our history as family. I do not know how I would have survived without that history—our working on our life together, not just with civility, but with care and good humor.

What a strange troupe we were that night, as Stuart took us for the very late flight to Las Vegas. I had never cared at all about going to Las Vegas.

Those first hours are blurred: The cab driver asking jovially what brought us to town. Our hope that it was not as bad as we all feared. The three of us talking to Mark, watching for some tiny response. We touched him. We listened to what they told us, but could barely take it in. I was terrified. You leaned against a wall, slid down to the floor, and put your head in your hands. Tracy was uncharacteristically quiet.

In the Family House we moved into a room—one room. It was not very big, and we were very tired. It was cold. We took turns sleeping and keeping watch.

As we went through those days, I thought back on the ways we have been family—more than just sharing responsibility for the boys. I thought about the ways we had learned to live with our brokenness, the ways we had found a new life together.

When someone broke into my house, it was you I called to board up the window. It was Tracy who called the next day and made me feel less crazy. "Somebody's been in your house and touched all your stuff." She understood.

And there was the night of the flood after the meeting at the boys' school. I was following you two and could see nothing but the taillights of your car. You were my lifeline. Tracy came and rode with me, and I was never so thankful for a companion in my car. We huddled together in that strange (very strange) man's kitchen until the storm subsided, and we could make our way home.

Many people died that night. I believe you and Tracy saved me.

One event stands for me as a paradigm for how we have been together. It was a Saturday morning at the boys' Little League game. Tracy and I had been talking about kids and work when a man listening to us said, "Are you two sisters?" Tracy paused, then answered, "No, I'm the stepmother of her two children." He just looked puzzled.

Are we sisters? No, we are the mothers of the same children. We love the same children.

As we huddled in the Family House during those dreadful days and nights, I remember how grateful I was for you and Tracy and the way we were together, loving the same children. I was thankful we could cry together and talk about the things that we wish we had done differently. I was thankful that we could find ways to laugh in the midst of the most devastating event in our lives. I was thankful we could all show our love to Mark and live our fear and grief in our own ways—and find support from one another. We took turns losing hope and holding steady.

What do families do who must go through such grief with anger and bitterness and alienation among them? Many have to. Some alienations must be too wide to heal. I have been cautious when people want to see us as a model. I could never explain how we did it. Were we lucky?

Yes. I also think we know something about forgiveness.

There is much I have forgotten, that I have chosen to forget, about the year of our divorce. The moment of forgiveness I have never forgotten: that moment when I asked if you would forgive me and you said I did not need to ask that, and I said I did, and you said yes. I dared to ask. I could not forgive myself. I did not know how to begin to ask God. I dared to ask, and in your "yes" I could begin again. It was your "yes" that made it possible for me to forgive as well—to forgive real or imagined hurts, intended

and unintended. ("Boys build houses. Girls clean houses.")
We could begin to shape something out of forgiveness.

I am thankful that the family we have shaped gave us
what we needed to live through Mark's death, to be there
for one another, and for David and Emily. I am thankful
that in the years of grieving, we have been able to talk and
make the decisions we had to make. Last summer, at
David and Maureen's wedding, there was comfort in
knowing that somebody else understood what bittersweet
meant.

We were a broken family, irretrievably broken. And in
ways I do not understand, the shattered pieces shaped
themselves into family again. It was not perfect. The broken pieces had sharp edges. We knew it was not perfect.
We did not pretend.

When Mark died, we were shattered again. This time we
had more help picking up the pieces. I did not know we
had so many friends. We could even smile about "celebrity
day" when Tracy got a call from her high-school friend Jill
Eickenberry, and you heard from Nick Lowery. But the television and football stars were, of course, the exception.
Our everyday friends and colleagues were there for us in
ways we could never have imagined.

Some say that parents of dead children are isolated. We
are too frightening for other parents. It might happen to
them. Do we have unusual friends? Is it that our lives in the
church have provided unusual friends?

Whatever the reasons, we had more help this time. We
had more help picking up the pieces. When we were broken before, few were there.

You said it poignantly and with uncommon candor at
your clergy retirement.

Calls, letters, visits, contributions from the bishop, superin-
tendents, colleagues, and former students were a force that
kept me from being completely overwhelmed by Mark's
death. But sixteen years earlier, when Susan and I were

going through a divorce, there were no calls, no letters, no visits. . . .

We did not have much help. Yet, as Hemingway put it, we grew strong in the broken places. We became family.

Shattered again, we all wondered if we could ever put pieces back together. Can any of us ever be whole? I do not know. The pieces will have to fit in peculiar ways, and the picture will not ever be complete again. But can we put them together? I believe we can, but I do not know.

We do know forgiveness.

As we cried together that day at the hospital, and confessed the ways we wished we had done things differently with Mark, I was asking again for forgiveness. By then, we knew we had forgiven each other. Now we had to be able to forgive ourselves.

We stand in a long line of those who have prayed a common prayer. Forgive us, we say, as we forgive. We believe the promise in the prayer. We believe we are forgiven, as we forgive. In truth, I believe we can *forgive* as we know we are *forgiven*. You helped me know that.

Can we put pieces together again?

What we call family—that peculiar constellation of you and Tracy, Emily, David and Maureen, Stuart and me—gives us a chance. Were we to live with the angers and alienations that infect many separated families, putting pieces together would be remote. How can there be a chance when it is the brokenness that is nourished? Do they know the prayer?

We know the prayer. That gives us a chance.

*Susan*

# To My Father

## Dear Daddy,

How did you know?

Mother said you did not sleep the night before Mark died. I wonder if I knew, in a way I could not touch, and you heard it and felt it and knew it. How you must have suffered, and you did it quietly, as you did everything. You loved Mark so. You radiated a gentle joy as you did things for him and the other grandchildren.

I know you loved me. You did that quietly too. I could not always read the signs, but I finally came to know how much you loved me. Mother wrote to me when I first went away to camp that you came home every day at noon to see if there was mail from me. How surprised I was. I had no idea it would matter so much to you.

A picture in my wedding album: You are reaching through the window of the car as Dick and I leave the church. You are holding my hand. I do not know the words to describe the look. Not sad, but a longing. The look of every father? Perhaps. It said to me how much you loved me.

I came to learn how important I was to you.

Then you wanted to protect me. You were reticent about Dick and me living in a parsonage next to the church in the middle of the city. You wanted me to be safe. You never wanted to see me hurt. You did your best.

Then came the accident. The vigil. Mark's death. December 16th. Sunday afternoon.

It was the Sunday that held for me the most treasured memories of growing up in Grace Church. It was the afternoon of the Candlelight Service. The anthem our choir sang every year is now in our hymnal. When I sing it now and come to what were always such strange words—"I-de-o, -o, -o"—my throat is tight and my heart returns to that grand sanctuary. I see shadows the candles throw against the gray walls. I feel the comfort, the assurance, that came with the readings—the gospel, the good news I knew even then by heart. The carols we sang together, and the wondrous anthems. Never, it seemed, was I ready for Christmas until that marvelous day. It was magic and sacred and holy.

A part of me was not surprised when I heard what you did that afternoon—that day you learned that your first grandchild was dead. You went to church. Mother stayed at home. Others were going to the service and came to get you. You went to church, to the Candlelight Service. You went to be in that sanctuary, to hear "I-de-o," to know the assurance that the stories were the same, and the news, in that place, was still good. *Ideo:* therefore. Christ is born. *Therefore*, glory to God! Christ is born to save us. *Therefore*, where else could you be?

In the midst of the worst any of us could imagine, you went to church. Without words, with the quiet, bent spirit with which you did everything in those last years, you went to church. And you were there for all of us.

Was it like the Palm Sunday forty years before, the day after your father died? I will not ever forget your broken voice on the telephone, "Papa's gone." The next morning you needed to go to church. Worship had not seemed very important to you before. The day after your father died, everything changed. Death does that; it changes everything. Was that the beginning of your intense seeking? Was that what led you to the deep and abiding faith that we saw and felt?

I think of the hours you spent each day, sitting in your big chair, reading your Bible, preparing the Sunday school lesson. In later years, when there were no longer lessons to teach, you were not through learning. You sat and read and thought. And I know you prayed. You did not talk much about praying. I just know you did it. What you were doing in that big chair, when you were able to do little else besides smile when the Cardinals scored, was praying—for, and on behalf of, all of us. I think of those convents full of sisters who never come out, who pray all the time. You would think they would finish. But, one said, there is never enough time for all the prayer that needs to be prayed. I think that was what you did for us. You did it that Sunday afternoon, when you went to the Candlelight Service. You did it every day. And in ways I do not understand, I believe you still do.

Was it a coincidence, or providence, that it was on All Saints' Day that your life ended here? You were hardly a saint. You, above all others, would deny that as foolishness. And yet, you pointed beyond yourself in ways you may never have understood.

Just a week after your memorial service, I went back to Grace Church to preach. I began with the words:

As I come to you this morning, my heart is full. It is filled with great joy and thanksgiving that I am honored to stand in this holy place, as one of your children, and bring a word of grace. And my heart is filled with sadness, for I covet the presence of those who no longer worship and witness in this earthbound sanctuary.

I often turn to comforting words in our *Book of Worship,* adapted from a Jewish memorial prayer. Let us pray together from these ancient words.

Everliving God,
    this day revives in us memories of loved ones who are with us no more.
The links of life are broken, but the links of love and long-ing cannot ever break.

We now see those we love with the eye of memory,
    their faults forgiven, their virtues grown larger.
So does goodness live, and weakness fade from sight.

Their lives are bound up in ours forever.
    Their memory is a blessing for us. Amen.

Hear our prayer, in the name of the one who came not to be ministered unto but to minister. Amen.

Goodness lives. Virtues grow larger. Your memory is a blessing for me.

Memory is strange. What makes it a blessing? Over the past few months I took time to write down memories of you. I wrote one down every day, because I sometimes have had trouble remembering all you have been for me.

I was always closer to Mother and, I have always thought, more influenced by her. I am like her in many ways. I look like her, I am told. I learned her strength and determination.

Yet, those close to us say I look like you and like Mom Sonnenday. I learned from both of you the blessing of quietness. I now know I learned from you what it means to pray and, maybe what is more important, the strength that comes when you pray for me.

I learned in those first weeks and months after Mark died that I was being carried by the prayers of the family of faith. There was a palpable sense of being carried. Some days I only moved through the day, I only moved from my bed, because I was being carried.

I know now that the prayers of the family of faith were grounded firmly in the closest part of that family. I know that you carried me and took care of me in the only way you could in those awful days. I know now that that is what you did all those years.

I do not have a book full of memories of things you have done. Everything you ever did for me, you did quietly, so there is much I may not remember. But you were there. And your prayers were there, and are there, and will be, always, unto the end of the age.

I love you, Daddy.

*S.*

# To My Mother

## Dear Mother,

For grandparents, there is a multiple grief. I know how you treasured Mark, your first grandchild. You were not too far away, so you could watch him grow. You and Daddy looked for opportunities to have him with you—and you did so many marvelous things for him. In each picture, he is likely to be wearing clothes you sent to him—the plaid jumpsuit he loved with the bear holding balloons or the tiny "grown-up" white shirt with "Mark" embroidered on the collar (which I have kept all these years, not yet finding another special Mark to wear it). And that magical trip when you took the boys to Disney World. I know how you loved him and what regard you had for his remarkable gifts. You delighted in him, and now he is gone.

I also see your grief for me. You came as fast as you could after he died. I can see you and Daddy and Aunt Kitty coming up the steps to the back door that Tuesday afternoon. When I asked how you were, you put your arms around me and said, "Now I'm all right." You do not show your sorrow and sadness very much, or very well. But those few words let me see your suffering for me heaped upon your grieving for Mark.

You had been steady through those days of vigil. I called you so early each morning. I was thankful you were up. No one else was. I ached to talk. I can see the place in the hospital hallway where I sat on the floor beneath the phone and leaned against the wall. I know each day you were praying to hear some good news, and I had none. You must have felt powerless—a thousand miles away and not a thing you could do for your own firstborn child. Just like me.

A multiple grief, for Mark and for me. I think, more than anyone, you have understood how hard it has been for me. Is it just because you are my mother?

More than that, you listen to me.

All those years you listened to me read a book report on Harriet Tubman, or try to find a rhyme for "peonies," or practice the Gettysburg Address. I sat up on the old red kitchen table while you peeled potatoes at the sink. And you listened.

It was not always easy. When I was fifteen and convinced I knew more about Robert E. Lee and Mideast politics and D. H. Lawrence than you could ever know, you still listened—and let me learn.

It was not always simple. When Mark was born and I became a mother, I found it harder to hear "You are just like your mother." I did not want to be just like my mother. I needed to be separate. I did not go through the rebellion many young people do in their teens. I managed to wait until I was thirty. It would have been better had I done it sooner.

I needed to be separate. I found myself blaming you for the parts of me I did not like. I sometimes heard your offers of help as judgment. I was not the perfect daughter you wanted me to be. I was not the perfect mother I wanted me to be.

I wanted to be my own kind of mother. I wonder if each generation of mothers swings pendulum-like away from what they resisted in their own mothers. I did not know how to tease out what was invaluable about how you loved me and what it was that was hard for me. I was desperately trying to mother Mark. I thought I knew what I did not want to do and be. I needed to be separate. That pain-filled and confusing time goes into the basket of regrets, the "what ifs" that every grieving mother shoulders.

Still, you listened. You tried to hear me.

I do not know what led me to Adrienne Rich. Her poetry was truth for me. Perhaps she knew something about mothering. She helped to heal me, and then we could begin to heal together. She helped me understand "motherhood as institution." I remember one woman, older than I, saying in exasperation, "There must be a school someplace where all mothers go, where they learn the same warnings, the same sighs, the same looks."

Of course there is a school. Its curriculum is woven into our cultures so tightly we cannot see the threads. Your mother learned it, and hers, and you. I learn it too.

Rich taught me that a mother believes she must communicate the hopes and expectations of the culture—for she knows what is needed for her child to survive. When I began to question those hopes, those expectations, I drew away from you. You had taught me. You had bonded tightly with me. To say no to what I found constricting, I drew away. In *Of Woman Born*, Adrienne Rich said it is "easier by far to . . . reject a mother outright than to see beyond her to the forces acting upon her." She is right.

I drew away, and in that moment of independence, of finding my own way, there was fear and ambivalence. I needed my mother. I wanted you to listen and understand what I could not understand.

You listened. I do not know that you always understood. You wrote me a letter in which you tried to understand, telling me how much you love me, just as I am, and I cried.

How thankful I am that we came through those hard times. How grateful I am that you persisted in your listening, in your trying to understand. I am thankful, too, for Adrienne Rich, for her wisdom that named my misplaced blaming.

How would I have lived this terror of mothering a dying child, of surviving as the mother of my dead child? How would I have lived without my mother mothering me? You listened and listened.

You ask me now how I am, in a way that is different from anyone else in the world. You call early in the morning each April 17th and December 16th—each birth-day and death-day. You sit, and drink coffee with me, and listen.

That afternoon, after Mark's memorial service, you asked if I wanted you to stay through Christmas, or go home and come back. I asked you please to leave, and please, come back. It feels strange now as I look back. Leave on Thursday. Come back five days later. I cannot even remember now why. Perhaps I needed to be alone, with Stuart, in my own house. What I most remember is that you listened. I was grateful.

That is why you understand. That is the way you know how hard it is. You listen.

You have also lived a long time. You have your own griefs—perhaps some I have never known or understood. You have rich friendships and stay connected with treasured colleagues throughout the world. Because you have loved widely and deeply, you know about grief.

Do you remember when Stuart gave me the delicate heart-shaped necklace? It was the first Christmas, nine days after Mark had died. The heart had an opening through which the chain went. You looked at it and whispered, "You will always have a hole in your heart." I remember your words each time I put it on. You know about grief, and then you knew more than I.

But I have learned. I have learned. During those times when it was getting worse, before it could begin to get better, I could have shielded you from how I was. I did not want it to be so hard for you. I did not want it to be so hard for anybody.

Could I have protected you? I do not know that it would have worked. Worse, you would have continued to feel powerless in the face of what you knew to be my suffering. And to feel powerless, helpless, not able to help your child, is a worse kind of pain. I know.

Sometimes there is nothing to do, and to live with that knowledge takes the kind of wisdom only years and suffering can teach. Then there are those moments when, in love and presence and care, you do more than you can know.

I wonder if grandparents are not often forgotten in the months and years following the death of the child they treasured. Your grief goes on, as mine does, and yours continues for Mark and for me. You keep listening. You ask and you listen.

I know now that I learned listening from you. I am beginning to discover, and to honor, how much I have learned from you. For so long, I needed to be separate. Now I add "Sonnenday" to my name. I still have to spell it for everyone, just as I did as a child. But I spell it with a quiet joy of being part of you and Daddy and all those mothers and fathers who have formed and shaped me—and you. I am separate, and we are together, because you listen.

As I practice anew what prayer can be, I have intimations of your listening. I know what it is to be heard.

I have often feared that parent images for God took me into perilous territory. How far all of us are, in our mothering and fathering, from who God is for us! As some began to talk of a mothering God, it frightened me. I wanted to say to my boys, "No. God is not like me. God loves you in ways I never could. Please do not confuse God's love and mine." I want to talk, instead, about all God *does*—with us and for us.

God listens. I know. I know what it means to be heard.

Please do not ever stop listening. Stay with me. Stay with others who know death and share with them the wisdom born of wounds. You can be with other grandmothers. You understand. You remember. You listen.

I love you.

*S.*

# More to My Wise Teacher

## Dear Bob,

As I wrote to you earlier, you taught me more than you will know. As I try to make sense of Mark's death, and continue my wandering in grief and confusion, I go back to what I learned with you.

My first year at DePauw, you taught Introduction to the New Testament. Not exactly your field. But you taught in a way so that I heard the gospel as *good* news. I learned what grace is. I learned grace from your profound understanding of Paul and the passion with which you gave witness to the Word.

At the time, it was an understanding that brought a sense of liberation, even deliverance.

Among my intense teenage memories is kneeling each Sunday evening at youth group worship in Crawford Chapel. I promised God I would try harder. And then the next Sunday evening, I would kneel again, and know I had failed. I had not been good enough. I would promise again.

I do not know why I did not *hear* grace then. I read it in scripture. I listened to sermons that proclaimed it. I sang the hymns of the Wesleyan tradition filled with the word. But I did not hear grace *for me*. Until New Testament 101. You taught grace. You preached grace. You taught me to exegete verse after verse until I came to know the amazing and unconditional grace we know in Christ Jesus.

Then you guided me into the world of Karl Barth. And grace abounded. One of the treasures of my college years was the trip to Chicago to hear Barth speak. I still have my notes and can put them beside the text of *Evangelical Theology*, and know that I truly heard him say those words. What radical grace, what assuring grace. Amazing grace, indeed.

The word of grace came as sheer gift to me in those years, long ago. Today, it is a blessing beyond measure. For I live in the assurance that Mark knows the blessing of grace even now. This week I read the Canticle of Remembrance from the Wisdom of Solomon.

> The souls of the righteous are in the hand of God
> and no torment will ever touch them.

The souls of the righteous. Mark would not have thought of himself as righteous—nor would many others. He was thoughtful—most of the time. He was loyal, defiantly loyal, to his friends. He had a way of caring for children that was splendid. His sister, Emily, adored him. His cousin Whitney still talks of the months he lived in Florida and the games they played. He was faithful in his way; he told me of stopping at a church to pray for our friend who was ill. That was two weeks before his accident.

Mark was a young man of many gifts. He used some of his gifts marvelously, and others lay waiting to be touched. He was impetuous and stubborn. He did not always use good judgment. Does that describe some of the rest of us at twenty-three? As our friend Sally said in the homily at the memorial service, most of us have another chance. Mark did not.

Many gifts. A charming and thoughtful and loyal young man. But, like most of us, not what the world would call righteous.

So I trust and give thanks that grace does abound for him this day, that he is counted as righteous through that mystery that is the life and work and death and resurrection of Jesus Christ. And it is by that grace that Mark lives in the arms of God.

Mark is neither righteous nor worthy. No one is, the psalmist writes. But, thanks be to God for the way in which, by grace, by the work of Christ, Mark is declared righteous, is worthy, does belong to God, is finally safe in God.

You brought me to life-changing truth. Nothing has been more important than the reality and power of grace. And in these awful days and months and years of grieving, the word of grace is the sustaining rock upon which I have begun to rebuild.

A woman called my office not long ago. Actually, she did not call *my* office. She called the seminary. It was one of those calls that no one else wants to touch. "Does your school teach universal salvation?" she asked. She wanted a yes-or-no answer. We began to talk.

She told me her church had a new pastor. He was preaching a gospel she did not recognize as "biblical enough." He implied that God could be bringing salvation to everyone. What will that do to guide our children? she worried. What if they are no longer *afraid* of not believing and not doing right? She concluded by asking, "Don't you believe in a real place called hell?"

I listened. I asked questions and listened. Then I gave witness to the word of grace I hear from Paul and Karl Barth and John Wesley, which you first helped me hear. That word of grace calls me to believe and gives me strength to act faithfully. It frees me from fear. I do not know how God will make decisions about all of us; that is in God's hands.

Then I had to tell her about Mark. I had to tell her. I said I was a mother whose son had died. I was a mother who did not have guarantees that my son had "confessed Jesus Christ as Lord and Savior" in just the way she believed one had to. I knew my son was not "righteous," as some would require for salvation. But I trust the promise. Nothing in all creation can separate any one of us from the love of God that we know in Christ Jesus. Grace is sufficient.

She was quiet. She had lost a child, a baby. He was in God's hands. She was sure. He was only a baby. And he had been baptized. But her friend had lost a grown son. She had not been back to church, for she agonized over her conviction that her son was not a Christian. He stood unworthy in the face of God's judgment. She had no hope.

I do not know how to encompass the paradox of scripture—listening with one ear to the parts the woman quoted with such conviction, and, with my heart, hearing the good news of great joy: grace is born into the world, and it is for all. I do not know how to preach as Wesley did—holding together what our minds see as incongruent. I only witness to the abundant words of grace I have come to know as the plumb line by which all other scripture is measured.

Grace. Amazing grace. What if you had not taught me? I would have no hope.

*Susan*

# *Dear Bob,*

Are you familiar with these words from an old hymn?

Does Jesus care when my heart is pained . . .
Does Jesus care when I've tried and failed . . .
Does Jesus care when I've said good-by
    To the dearest on earth to me . . .

    O yes, He cares; I know He cares,
His heart is touched with my grief;
When the days are weary, the long nights dreary,
I know my Savior cares.

A friend gave the words to me the day of Mark's memorial service. I have kept them in my prayer list book and many mornings read them, over and over.

Does Jesus care when I've said "good-by" to the dearest on earth to me? When there's a hole in my heart . . . and life? When memories bring the question, "Have I tried . . . and failed?"

The days grow weary, so weary. No one told me I could be this tired. Is that what "dead-tired" means? Bone-weary. Spent, through and through. And long, long, dreary nights. Everything gray and fog-filled.

I keep hearing a line from Annie Dillard's novel *The Living*. Young Hugh, who watched his father die in a logging accident stands quietly at the graveside. As he hears the minister thunder, "O Death, where is thy sting?" the boy responds to himself, "Just about everywhere, since you ask."

Just about everywhere.

In those early days after Mark died, everywhere I turned, there were memories. There were the good memories I cherished. I remember the morning Mark was born. I looked out the window at the budding trees in the park and knew at last what folks meant when they said, "All is right with the world." I remember quiet afternoons in the parsonage, holding him, nursing him, loving him. All is right. He grew older, and there was the day we cleaned out the closet in the front bedroom, and he organized *everything*. And then the early morning of golf in Scotland—a highlight of his life to play at 5:00 A.M., in the rain, at St. Andrew's Old Course.

I remember the meal together after David's graduation— our family's last supper, it turned out to be. And the phone call that he had completed his drive across the country by himself. He was in California. He was safe.

Such good memories they had been. But their significance had always been connected with looking forward, anticipating another chapter. And now, there are no more chapters.

Death, where is thy sting? Just about everywhere, since you ask.

What of the hard memories, the bad times? The sting of death reshapes these into the "what ifs" of every loss. I cannot forget the day I pushed two-year-old Mark away to "go play" so I could feed his new baby brother, and striking him once in a moment of frustration and anger. Later there was the end of the marriage. As Dick and I sat at the table to tell the boys, the younger spoke his five-year-old anger, "If you are going to tell us you are getting divorced, I'm going to hit you." Honest and clean and clear. But Mark carried his pain in silence. As I watched his hurt, I kept wondering if I had tried hard enough to make the marriage work. Had I quit too soon—and injured everyone I loved?

And I will not forget the telephone call when I did not have time to talk. That telephone call. I was on my way out the door, and Mark did not tell me he was getting ready to leave, to take a short trip. He did not tell me—and I did not have time to talk. I did not take time to talk. And he left. And he drove. And he died.

The sting. Just about everywhere. Mark's death adds a

poignant, bittersweet flavor to the good of the past, and leaves the bad with no more opportunities to go back, to redeem the hurt.

> Does Jesus care? Does Jesus care?
> When I have lost the dearest on earth to me?
> When I know I have failed—

and am haunted by, "what if, what if . . ."?

The words follow with such assurance, and without answers or solutions.

> I know my Savior cares,
> His heart is touched with my grief.

I grow weary of those who want to bring answers and assurances that there was nothing I could have done differently. I am not comforted by someone else's confidence that I did the best I could at the time.

Of course I could have done things differently. I could have been a better mother. I did not always say "yes" at the right times, or "no" when "no" was needed. I was more attentive to my own wants during those awful and wonder-full and confusing years of the 1960s and early 1970s.

Even among the most responsible, who is ever ready to be a parent? As one wise person mused, "It is not parents who create children, but children who create parents." And by the time we figured it out, the next chapter was beginning, and we had to be created anew.

Of course I could have done it differently—and better. God knows! Yes. God knows. And cares. And in Christ Jesus does not just say it is all right. The old hymn says "I know He cares, His heart is touched with my grief"—the grief of mistakes, the grief of times of alienation, the grief of no more chances, the grief of death.

Where is thy sting? Just about everywhere. And yet, the

promise of care, the assurance that Jesus knows my grief, lives beside the everywhere sting.

I want no premature consolation. It is not fine. It is awful. And to pretend that it is all right, that it will ever be *all* right, is to deny how I know it was, how I know I was through all those years. It is to deny the way in which good memories and bad history take on a new sting in the face of death. There are no more chances, with Mark, to redeem the mistakes.

But Jesus cares. And for now, let that be enough. Let the sting exhaust its power. I will not pretend right now that I am fine.

Jesus cares. I know he cares. His heart is touched with my grief.

Death, where is thy sting? Right now, just about everywhere. But it is not borne alone.

Blessings,

*Susan*

Three years later

*Dear Bob,*

I have just reread a copy of a letter I sent you—the one fraught with guilt and the sting that is "just about everywhere." It is not surprising. They say that guilt is a parent's most pervasive response when a child dies. I have never found comfort in discovering I am like everybody else; yet, it may be time for me to listen.

I could not revisit the awful guilt were it not for what you taught me about grace. Is there a word of grace—even for me? Even now? I wrote to you that I did not find help in premature consolation, in some kind of assurance that I did the best I could as Mark's mother. I know I could have done it differently. I could have done it better.

Premature consolation. Is that what Dietrich Bonhoeffer meant by "cheap grace"? Just say that everything is fine, and it will be. Is that what I have been resisting? Is my "living with the sting" a kind of refining fire? A self-imposed "tough love"? Or is it also a stubborn refusal to hear a word of grace? To trust a promise of forgiveness?

The Christmas after Mark died, my friend Jean sent me a Christmas blessing:

> May these days of Christmas festival
>   bring you, in your suffering,
> I do not say consolation,
>   but the blessing God intends for you.
> The Child Jesus will perhaps not give
>   you any sweetness,—
> he reserves that for the weak ones,—
> but his hands will none the less be spread
>   to bless you . . .
> and whether you feel it or no,
> he will pour abundant grace into your soul.
>
> Charles de Foucauld in<br>*Meditations of a Hermit*

Every year since, I have shared the blessing with others who are grieving. Just yesterday, one to whom I had sent it thanked me and said she had lost count of the number of others to whom she had sent it. It speaks to many hearts, as it does to mine.

I wonder if it speaks so tenderly to us because it acknowledges the trouble we have trusting that grace is being poured into us—whether we feel it or not. Is there still, deep within the psyche of others besides me, that gnawing pagan sense that if I had been better, done better, this would not have happened? That sense of guilt and responsibility for whatever bad has come? Even those closest to the incarnation of grace must have felt it, "Rabbi, who sinned, this man or his parents, that he was born blind?"

I do know I could have been better, done better. I know the sin of my own self-centeredness. I could have been a better mother—a much better mother. I know all of that. And I also know the promise of the Christmas blessing. It is not consolation, premature or otherwise. It is, rather, the blessing that God intends for me. It is grace, abundant grace, day after day, poured into my soul, whether I feel it or not.

It is the grace you taught me. It is the grace by which Mark lives in the arms of God. Radical grace, assuring grace. Amazing grace.

And it may be only as I stand in the assurance of that abundant grace that I am able to name the sting as guilt. Only as I know that overpowering gift of forgiveness, and see anew what God has done in the Child-Man Jesus, am I able to confess the ways in which I know I have fallen short of God's will for my life. I think that is close to what Karl Barth taught me. Only in the light of God's work in Christ do I know who I am, what I am, what I have done—and not done. And then I can begin to pray,

> Let me now accept thy forgiveness and forgive myself. . . . No atonement of mine, no expiation or propitiation, is possible or necessary. Thou dost not ask me to atone but to accept freedom from the burden of guilt, so that the forgiven past becomes an asset in a dedicated future.

The forgiven past—an asset in a dedicated future. Forgive and forget? No. Forgive and remember. God knows, and never forgets, who I am, who I have been, what I have done—and not done. God knows. God remembers. And, with abundant and amazing grace, God forgives.

A forgiven past. Not a forgotten past.

A forgiven past. An asset. A dedicated future. A future dedicated to proclaiming the good news of great joy that the Child Jesus, whether you feel it or not, is pouring abundant grace into each soul. Sins are forgiven. The blind see. Every tear is wiped away, and sorrow and sighing, finally, will flee.

A forgiven past, still filled with regrets, sadness, "what ifs." But the burden of guilt lifts as the Child Jesus pours abundant grace day after day after day after day. And it is an asset in a dedicated future. It is an opportunity to look forward, without the fear of abandoning all that is past, without the fear of forgetting the bad times and the good. It is an invitation to go on.

A forgiven past is the beginning of new life—in the name of the One who has come that we may have life and have it with abundant grace. My wise teacher, you have taught me well. I thank God for you.

My prayers,

*Susan*

# To Our Nurses

## To you who cared for Mark—

Thank you.

When Mark died, I tried to thank you for all you had done for him, for us. I fear I was not very clear about many things then. I must tell you—clearly.

I do not know how you live your lives, do what you do, day after tragic day. Head injuries. What could be more traumatic, more confusing? One of you said that, if you knew when you started what you know now, you never would have become involved with the unit. But now you have so much experience, it was not right to leave. You stay. Day after tragic day.

Of all you did for us, the most valuable was your telling the truth. You told us what was happening and what that meant—always careful to add that there is much no one can know. And you cared for Mark and for us with such delicate skill and wisdom.

That first morning, I came to the room very early. I learned more than I wish I ever had reason to know about voluntary and involuntary movements. The way Mark moved his leg you called "posturing." He was not doing it on purpose. It did not mean he was conscious. Posturing. I have never again been able to use that word to describe that pretentious way some people act. Posturing. When I hear someone else say it, I see Mark, his leg slightly bent, lifted above the bed. Nothing pretentious. Involuntary. Unconscious. Entirely unconscious.

I learned about the uncertainties of recovery, and what it means for parts of a brain to die. I learned that there was no way to know if Mark would survive and, if he did, how he would be. You told us about recoveries that seemed like miracles, and you were clear that there were times when there was no miracle, no healing—even if life continued.

You played music for Mark. You shaved the stubbly beard on his chin and cheeks. You talked to him, clearly and directly, as if he could understand. You told us to talk to him, how important it was. Maybe he could hear. Perhaps he could understand. The sound of our voices was important, just as with a newborn. Just like a newborn. I remembered my newborn babies and recoiled at Mark as a baby again, a twenty-three-year-old with the understanding of a baby.

You told us the truth.

I remember when one of you came back after being off for a couple of days. You said, "They *have* told you he is worse, haven't they?" Yes. The others had been clear. They told us the truth. He was worse.

You listened to us and talked to us. You told us enough about *you* for us to appreciate how and why you can do this. One of you told me it had been just a year since the one you loved most had died in an accident, and I could begin to understand why we felt close to you. As you stood beside me on that Sunday afternoon, while the doctor declared Mark brain-dead, I knew you understood. You did not need to say a word.

Now, with the perspective of years, I see how you and I

and others wounded in grief must find ways to stand with those freshly wounded. Could all of our suffering have been in vain? Is there not something "to do with it"? Surely all is vanity, unless we can carry our grief into a transforming presence with others who weep. You may not say it that way, but you did it that way.

As the staff changed for the weekend, one of you left your home telephone number. It was another intimation that you did not anticipate that Mark would be there when you returned. I do not know if you can understand how important it was for me to be able to call you and tell you Mark had died and to try to thank you.

You said then how terrible his injuries had been, how you had never seen a CAT scan like that. It helped me know that we could not have wished for him to live. It was a confirmation that the doctor could do no other but to say what we knew—Mark was dead. The Mark we knew and loved was dead the moment his head was damaged in the accident.

During one of those long afternoons, as one of you let me stay longer than the rules said I was supposed to, I talked with Mark and stroked his body. You and I talked. You were not a part of any faith community. I had a sense that you did not have much regard for "organized religion." And yet, you are part of my faith community. God worked through you in our lives, in ways you may not understand or even like to think about.

In my work, we sometimes struggle with the language of "professionalism." Is the ministry a profession? Does that connote an absence of care or availability, a lack of compassion or vulnerability?

I think of you, all of you. Competency. Skill. Insight. Experience. The consummate professionals. And also the fact that you grieved your own griefs with me. You opened your private time to me. You tended to Mark with a gentle touch I could only call love. Compassion and vulnerability.

Caring and presence. The consummate professionals. You have shown us what "professional" means.

You began our journey toward our changed lives with your care and wisdom and truth. I left the hospital that day without "what ifs" concerning Mark's care. As does every mother, I will always have "what ifs" about his life and death, but not about his care during those seven days. I left you believing that all that could have been done was done, and his healing simply could not come in the way we had hoped.

Because of you, Mark lived his last days with skilled and loving hands carrying him, offering tenderness as well as treatment. Because of you, he died with dignity—the dignity of the sacred child of God he was created to be.

Thank you.

Warmest regards,

*Susan Vogel*

# To My Friend Sally

## Dear Sally,

"So, here we are," you began. "None of us planned for this event. Mark's accident and death were not written into our calendars. Perhaps the greatest hope and assurance in this time is we are not alone. We have one another to cry with, to rage with, to sit with together in silence."

What happened for me in that memorial service, in that worship of remembering, will always be linked with you, my dear friend. My dear friend. My trusted colleague. My brilliant student. What a curious set of relationships we crafted over the years.

"We are not alone," you preached that day. I gave thanks for the ways in which we have been together, for each other.

It was many lives ago when you came to seminary. I learned you had long lived with pain. You were very young. But you knew You knew more about pain and hardship and grief than I did. When you were in school, I wanted you to feel safe. You knew better. You knew the world was not a safe place.

I watched as you grew in ministry, and you became my trusted colleague and wise friend.

Then (do you remember?) we were asked to plan worship for a pastors' school. We agreed that you would sing, and together we would move into liturgical dance with words from Isaiah. (You were not sure about the liturgical dance part.)

> I will never forget you, my people;
>  I have carved you on the palm of my hand.
> I will never forget you;
> I will not leave you orphaned.
> I will never forget my own.

Side by side we moved, reaching toward the congregation, and then gathering them in toward our hearts. The next stanza began

> Does a mother forget her baby?
>  Or a woman the child within her womb?
> Yet even if these forget, yes, even if these forget,
>  I will never forget my own.*

As we "cradled babies" in our arms and then turned away from them, you moved behind me and encircled me as I rocked the baby only I could feel. I felt a deep ache for my babies, now grown to young men. I remembered cradling them. I remember the aching, yearning love I felt in those moments of holding and rocking. At the same time, I felt the comfort of being cradled and rocked.

Cradled and rocked. Cradling and rocking.

Can God love me that way? Does God gather me and hold me, cradle and rock me? In those moments, God acted in and with you to be a presence I discovered as steadfast and mothering.

Who else, then, could be with me, for me, in the worst days of my life? Who else was wise enough about grief and pain, cradling and rocking?

You came. You listened. You heard.

When you spoke at Mark's memorial service, your words were true. You described the Mark who was real to us. You named his marvelous gifts, and you did not leave out his idiosyncrasies and his demons. You spoke to each of us, for each of us. You reminded us that in his unsettled-ness, Mark was similar to many of us when we were twenty-three. We grieved that he did not get another chance.

Naked with our pain, you said, we wonder how to make it through. But I was not yet face-to-face and naked with my pain. I was too dead inside. I did not yet know what it was to feel naked with pain. Later I learned, again and again. And I will never forget the words with which you ended: your offering toward how to make it through. You stepped back from the pulpit. You looked at all of us. You began to sing.

> I will never forget you, my people;
>> I have carved you on the palm of my hand.
> I will never forget you;
> I will not leave you orphaned.
>> I will never forget my own.

You sang. All was silent. You sat down. We listened to the silence. And in the silence, I heard what you did not sing that day:

> Does a mother forget her baby?
>> Or a woman the child within her womb?
> Yet even if these forget, yes, even if these forget,
>> I will never forget my own.

I was cradling and rocking, cradled and rocked. I was cradling and rocking my baby, my firstborn child. And around us, rocking us and cradling us, are the arms of the One who will not leave us orphaned, who will never, never forget.

Thanks be to that One who has blessed me with my wise and trusted friend,

*Susan*

# To Perry, Trusted Colleague

Fall 2000

## Dear Perry,

I discovered last week that you had left ordained ministry. I grieve our loss, the church's loss. The gifts you brought to ministry nourished us generously.

I never adequately thanked you for helping lead Mark's service. I could never adequately thank you. You did it with your rare wedding of gentleness and confidence-inspiring strength. I had seen that often, especially at Pineridge House.

Pineridge House. I am thankful that you came to see this Sunday afternoon Communion ministry as yours too. What a distinctive group of people gathered for worship in that boarding-home community: Kevin, who could tell us each date—for years ahead—when we were due for our every-other-week visit. (He reminded me that in 1967, April 17th, the day Mark was born, was a Monday.) Mike, with unseeing eyes, waiting with cupped hand for bread, and Orville, nodding reverently as he received the juice, whispering, "Thank you, ma'am."

It has been as rare a calling as any I know. My own life has known painful and joyous transitions. But Sunday afternoon Communion has been constant. Every other Sunday. Twenty-six years. A calling I never anticipated, could never explain, and am reluctant to relinquish. A sanctuary of circled chairs beside the piano with the kitchen noises in the background. Many ages and cultures gathered, each with a story to tell and challenges to face.

As we came together, you were at home with each person, and they with you. When Richard was agitated, and his foot bounced harder and harder, you spoke softly to him, and he settled a bit. As Josh came in, walking like an aging Michael Jordan, you knew how to ask how the Chiefs game was going and how to listen for whether he had heard from his grandson. Whenever Mabel was upset because someone else had the yellow-covered songbook, you skillfully exchanged yours for the yellow one, and passed Mabel's treasured, if temporary, possession to her.

I watched you and was thankful. I was no longer anxious when I was out of town, because I knew you would be there to do the service. You and I both knew the importance of the continuity that together we provided, continuity in lives that were often disjointed, discontinuous. You were there for me and for our curious and blessed flock.

And so I needed you with us on that dreaded funeral day. God worked in you, and we were thankful. Then we had to figure out how to go on with our lives.

I went back to Pineridge the next Communion Sunday. I do not remember much. I am sure you said you would do the service if I wanted you to. But I needed to do it. I needed to figure out how to go on with my life. For more Sundays than I could count (though our Pineridge savant, Kevin, could tell us), I had celebrated Communion in the midst of that circle. I needed to be there.

At the time for sharing our prayer concerns, I began to thank everyone for their care and for praying for us. Do you remember, as soon as I spoke of Mark's death, how that man came to me? He took hold of my arm and knelt beside me. (My memory is that he looked like Kramer on *Seinfeld*, doing what Kramer might have done.)

What happened next is fuzzy. (Many days and months are fuzzy.) I know he was saying how sorry he was. He was trying to bring comfort. In that place where I thought I was the caregiver, he knew I needed care. People do not know what to do with grieving parents. But this Kramer-like man did what he knew to do. He knelt beside me and offered his care.

You may not have realized how your confidence-inspiring presence made me feel steady in those moments. I thanked the kneeling man, and we went on. We went on through weeks and months. You were there when I needed you, but you encouraged me to go on. What ministry I came to know from you and those others to whom I thought I was ministering.

One afternoon I greeted a young, weary-looking man, told him my name and asked his. "William," he whispered hoarsely. Later, having said our usual words about using grape juice "so all may share in the bread and the cup," I came to him. "William, this is the blood of Christ." He shook his head. "Better not." "It *is* grape juice," I repeated. And he responded, "You just don't know what it might turn into."

You just don't know what it might turn into. William was right: A miracle. A mystery. Each time we gather around that table, you just don't know what it might turn into.

As different as we are from one another, as separated or divided as we may become from one another, we are bonded together as one, for we all share in the Body of Christ. This *is* the Body of Christ, and it is broken for *all* of us.

You just don't know.

Look at the way this disparate body of believers in this unlikely place has been bonded together as one. Look at those who, some would say, live on the margins. Look at how they care for those of us who know ourselves privileged in the things of the world. Look and see how they love one another. Look at how they have loved me back into life.

After you moved back to California, I was sad to lose contact with you. Then early this fall, I was looking at a collection of clergy stoles and saw your name. I saw your stole with the words that you had left United Methodist ministry. It was the "Shower of Stoles" that reflects divisions in our church. I saw one belonging to a man who had died following his struggle with AIDS and one from a father who grieved over his lesbian daughter experiencing no home in the church. I saw one with a bishop's symbol. I saw yours, and I grieved our loss, the church's loss.

Perry, my friend, I will never be able to thank you for the ways you were here for me in the worst of times. I also give thanks that you knew what it was to be bonded together as one with this little body of believers at Pineridge and live in mutual love. I know one reason that this ministry was a blessing in your life: You have known what it is like to live on what some see as margins. You are one of those precious ones who, out of that experience, live not in bitterness but with a compassion that overflows abundantly and a hope that someday it will be different.

William was right—about all things ordinary and sacred. You just don't know what it will turn into. Each time we gather around that table, you just don't know. As different as we are from one another, as separated or divided as we may become from one another, we are bonded together as one, for we all share in the Body of Christ.

This *is* the Body of Christ, and it is broken for *all* of us.

You just don't know.

My prayers,

*Susan*

# To Faithful Jean

## Dear Jean,

When I consider prayer, I think of you. You live in prayer in a way I could not understand.

Years ago, while you were teaching at Saint Paul, twelve women sat in a circle, intrigued with the notion that how we did pastoral counseling might be "different." You described how you prepared when someone asked for counseling. Knowing your writing in feminist theology, and the breadth of your scholarship, we waited for your guidance. You spoke of your reticence about your own wisdom, despite many years of study and practice. You said that you begin: "Jesus, I cannot do this myself. I need you to sit here beside me."

I felt wonder as I listened to you. It was not what we expected to hear. You began with praying, you said. I could tell you meant it. You took days for prayer retreats. You live in prayer.

I did not understand. And then Mark died.

On the first anniversary of his accident, I spoke to the seminary community as they gathered for the noon meal.

> One year ago my son Mark died. I come today to thank you for taking time to pray for me—during the shock of loss and all of the days since. We are able to continue our lives only because God has worked through the prayers of the community of faith to carry us.
>
> I wrote to you last January saying that, someday, perhaps, I would be able to find ways to let you know how important your prayers have been and to find a way to thank you. It now is clear: The way we thank one another is to promise to pray for one another—and to mean it. The road is long. Let us promise to pray for one another.

During that year I had begun to learn what it means to pray. You will look surprised. I have always been in a family and a community that prays. I grew up with grace at mealtime. I prayed in church: I confessed what I fear were often someone else's sins; I was strengthened by pastoral prayers that bound our beloved congregation together; I have spent uncounted moments at the altar rail when I promised God I would try harder and do better. When it was "time to pray," I did.

I often said the words, "You're in my prayers," when what I meant was, "I am thinking of you and I care about you in your time of trouble." Others said it to me. A woman was once so angry with me that she raged, "I'm going to pray for you." A threat, an insult. How had the image of prayer grown so distorted?

I had students who promised that I was on their prayer list, and wanted to be sure they knew Mark and David's names. A prayer list. That was as hard for me to comprehend as an angry woman's taunt. Both were part of worlds' I did not know.

On that December Sunday, it changed. I had often brought student concerns to the community meal for prayer, but now the community sent word that it was Mark for whom they were praying. The woman at the Las Vegas store where I bought tennis shoes listened tenderly to me talk about Mark, and when I stopped by again, she told me she had put Mark's name on her church prayer chain.

The card on the flowers from Kirk said simply, "I am praying."

When I went to the hospital chapel and knelt at that altar rail, the position felt familiar, but there were no words. I sensed what Paul must have meant: the Spirit praying, with sighs too deep for words. Mark and I were being carried by all those prayers from communities of faithful people. And my own voiceless prayers were being carried too.

Mark died, and I returned home.

The notes and telephone calls said it again and again. "We are praying for you." Some sounded much like what I had meant so often: "I'm thinking of you. I care." And I was thankful. And yet, some had a specificity that made me know that, yes, they were *praying* for me.

"At the breakfast table this morning, we lifted up you and Mark and your family."

"When we had our devotions tonight, the children said your names first."

In those promises of prayer I heard power I had not known. There was a palpable sense of being carried by the prayers of dozens of intertwining communities and people of faith. While I was too broken and exhausted and confused to know what or how to pray, the Spirit—through those faithful ones—was praying in and for us. This change has nothing to do with explaining or understanding. Prayer remains among the mysteries before which I am in awe. I simply witness to the sustaining power I know.

So it is that, having experienced the work of the Spirit through the prayers of the people, many people, I knew myself to be one called to pray for others. These people of prayer kept me alive, a magnificent thing for which I know not how to say thank you enough. Now I wanted to pray. I needed to pray.

Knowing my "human condition" requires discipline, and perhaps also because I am a child of John Wesley, I needed a method, an order. I had heard others talk of prayer lists. I never had one. Now I needed one. I wanted one.

Carefully tucked in a drawer of special gifts was a small book, the cover swirled with red and green, yellow and blue. Inside were lined pages, waiting. You sent it to me for Christmas from Zimbabwe.

I began a prayer list.

*February 5, 1991*

*Mark*

Mark is first. How do I pray for Mark? I was not sure how to begin. I began with tears. "God, please. Hold him. Hold him in your love. Hold him tight. He is safe with you." I was holding tight to what Paul had said. Whether we live, or whether we die, we are the Lord's. I pray that in whatever ways Mark knows, he knows how completely we love him.

Mark is first.

Then the others dearest to me—
*David*
*Stuart*
*Mother and Daddy*
Then *Fritz and Etta Mae*
They suffered the death of one son from AIDS a week after Mark died, and would know the death of a second son nine months later. I pray for Tim and Fred, for their brother, Marty, and for the witness their parents bring as they tell their story.
*Sam, Pat, Margaret and Jim, Dick and Rick*

They had just watched sons leave for the Gulf War. Their terror of the unknown seemed somehow harder to bear than our known grief.

The list grows each day. My childhood pastor is dying. A young friend who had been critically ill is better, but they are not sure what was, or is, wrong. Uncle Ed has died. Marshall and Cindy are expecting a baby. My minister, campaigning for mayor, faces thinly disguised racist attacks. You have written that your mother is not well, and "Jean and Florence" are on the second page.

Each morning I open the book and speak each name. I speak with thanksgiving for God's presence through this time of suffering, or words of petition, begging that the cup pass from this one who is on my heart. How do you ever cross a name off the list? A crisis may pass. The loss becomes less raw. But I am bonded into a forever covenant with sisters and brothers for whom I pray. So the list grows longer.

The crisis may not pass. A friend's son knows a life of depression, then closes the windows and turns on the gas. Our dear friend has faced demonic addiction, and finally a time of recovering has come, but the ravages of the years have caused irreparable damage. Another friend hears a diagnosis of AIDS, and another, and another. Three more dead sons. And a daughter—tiny, not-ready-to-be-born, already loved, Grace. How do I stop praying for mothers and fathers whose grief parallels my own? In those early times, I was beginning to suspect that the road would be very long. I knew that they, we, would not be "just fine" very soon.

I was learning about time and grief and healing, and each day I wanted to speak the names of those in that company of grieving parents, that company in which we had begged not to be included.

A crisis may pass, but what else may enter into the lives of those to whom I am bound in prayer? Our retired colleague—one for whom you have such fondness too—flies across the country to face his son's critical illness. "I took a dark suit," he said. With the miracle of his son's healing, our prayers turned to thanksgiving. And then a grandson came into their home. Grandparents parenting again. So many prayed for him, for them.

How do I ever cross someone off the list? I can begin to understand the need for those blessed orders of sisters and brothers who spend their lives in prayer. There is so much for which to pray. How does one bring an order to the calling?

After a time, I prayed for a portion of the list each day. My friend smiles when I remind her that she is on my "Wednesday list," a day she faces difficult meetings. I pray the pages for this day, and also for others whose struggles are critical. Then comes the glorious moment when anguished weeks of prayer for another threatened pregnancy are transformed into psalms of joy and thanksgiving for birth and new, healthy life. Joshua is here. He is well. Praise be to God.

I pray. Each morning I pray. The list continues to grow, but the book has many pages. There is still room. How could I ever take anyone off the list?

I am bonded into a forever covenant with sisters and brothers for whom I pray. Their lives are intertwined with mine, and they can never again become strangers.

Not long ago, I paused at the name of our friend—the one who had packed his dark suit when he feared his son was dying. I had been out of touch. I called and discovered the continuing challenges of illness their family must face in their senior years. His voice was thin, sad. "It sounds like a hard time," I said. He was quiet a moment, then answered, "Yes, and you know about hard times."

Bonded into a forever covenant with sisters and brothers for whom I pray, and who continue to carry me with their prayerful care. Our lives are intertwined. How could I ever take anyone off the list?

I have been given a new life. And the new life has a center in prayer that I did not know was possible. I know you understand. You showed me.

Friendship always,

*Susan*


*Dear Jean,*

I have a prayer problem. I thought first of you. Will you help me?

It is not about how prayer works or if God listens—or cares. I know that is what some wonder. There are grieving parents who never pray again. "It did not prevent the worst thing in our lives," they say. "Why would we ever pray again?"

Those are not my questions or doubts. I do not need to understand. Prayer remains mystery. I pray because of the way I have been carried by the prayers of intertwined communities of faith. Because of what these generous people of prayer have done for me, I must pray for others who know trouble. I must pray especially for those who are grieving. My problem is what comes after prayer.

What does it mean when Jesus says to go into your closet to pray? To pray in secret? When he talks of acts of love, what does it mean not to let the right hand know what the left hand is doing? How do these admonitions apply to all those generous people who told me, who keep telling me, that they are praying for me? My problem is, how do these admonitions apply to me?

I am unlikely to be declaiming in the sanctuary or standing on street corners. That comes not from virtue but my own constricted tradition and history. I find it hard even to go to the altar rail to pray with other people watching. I am most at peace doing my praying in secret, early in the morning. A singular peace comes on days I can sit outdoors in the dark stillness, watch the stars, then the streaking pink across the sky. I know comfort in the assurance that I pray as part of the community of faith, even when I pretend I am alone. I covet the praying in secret.

But then, I cannot make myself keep it secret. I must tell.

When I was first stricken and helpless, there was a palpable sense of being carried by the prayers of dozens of intertwining communities and people of faith. I knew they were praying. They told me. While I was too broken and exhausted and confused to know what or how to pray, the Spirit—through those faithful ones—was praying in and for us. I knew they were praying, because they told me. These people of prayer kept me alive.

Having experienced the work of the Spirit through the prayers of the people, many people, I knew I was called to pray for others. How will they know if I do not tell them? People of prayer carried me and kept me alive. I can do no other.

I tell them. I write letters and make telephone calls. I wrap my arms around them and whisper the words. I take their hands and promise I am praying. I send e-mail messages, though that still feels incongruous. I wonder why? Do I doubt that our God of flaming bushes and astounding births can work through incomprehensible technology?

In my prayer book are dates—dying dates, birthing dates, times I know to be hard for others. Jerome's death date sits next to his father's birthday; and Jerome's birth date, six days before Christmas. I have learned. These are times I tell his father and brother how much I am praying for them. It has been seven years. They go on with their lives, most of the time. But there are moments, and some moments last a season. Mid-March. Christmastime.

How can I not tell them? I want them to know they are

remembered. People of faith remember and pray for one another. So many do not remember. They think we are fine. They see us working and laughing. They think we must have moved through all those mythical "stages" and now we are fine. But they do not understand. They do not know that we wake up every morning and say, "I wonder how it will be today."

Praying in secret? The praying may be in secret, but I cannot leave it there. I know the palpable sense of being carried by the prayers of dozens of intertwining communities and people of faith, because they told me. Is that not what I am called to do? I could say, "Paul did it." I should do it because Paul did it. In each letter he wrote, Paul told those first Christians that he was praying for them. He asked them to pray for him and for one another. Surely he had heard the admonitions about praying in secret. Still he reminded the people of his prayers each time he spoke with them.

You may shake your head and wonder why I ask these questions. Maybe it is because this all seems new to me. So much changed when Mark died. Everything changed when Mark died. I believe the prayers of God's people kept me alive. I am called to pray, and I want to do it faithfully.

I also have seen what some parts of the church, and some outside the church, have done with and to prayer. It has been abused and misused. I want to do it faithfully.

I received a call once from an older friend. "I am calling from the hospital. I had a little heart attack and am waiting for some tests. You don't need to come over. I don't want to spread the word around. I am okay. Just thought maybe a little prayer would be fine."

Then his voice broke. "I really am all right," he assured me. A little heart attack. A little prayer would be fine. I tell him each time we talk that I pray for him, because his family has faced some hard times. So he called me to pray for him.

I know I do not pray as often as many do. I have not

studied much of the history and theology and practices of prayer. I am not a better pray-er than somebody else. I do tell people when I am praying for them. So I am the one my friend calls: "Just thought maybe a little prayer would be fine."

Why don't more people do that? Maybe they do not know what it means to feel broken and helpless, and to hear that someone else is carrying them in prayer. Maybe they believe they are supposed to keep it secret. Maybe I am supposed to keep it secret. But I cannot do that. I know that the prayers of faithful people kept me alive. They told me. Would their prayers have kept me alive had they not told me?

I do not know. There are those for whom I continue to pray who may not know I do. I pray for many who have died, beginning with Mark. I pray that they may know the assurance that they are not forgotten. I pray for those far away, with whom I am rarely in contact and those to whom I cannot write: The part of our family that does not want to be found and the troubled child in a foster home. I pray for my once-brilliant student whose brain is irreparably damaged. I pray for friends of friends, whom I will never know; I pray because my friends ask me to.

What does that mean?

I am clear that I do not understand how prayer works. I am troubled using the language of prayer "working." I scoff at studies that try to measure the power of prayer, when people do not know others are praying for them.

Prayer remains for me one of God's many mysteries. And so also, perhaps, is what comes after prayer. To tell or not to tell? Perhaps it is not a problem. It is part of the mystery.

I tell, and whatever else happens is mystery in God's hands. When I cannot tell, whatever else happens is mystery in God's hands. You will understand that also.

With prayers,

*Susan*

# To My Young Friend Who Knows Healing

Have you any idea how we rejoice in you and your life? You were at the edge of lost. Now you are found and whole. How glad was the woman who found even a lost coin! How much more the shepherd who feared for his lamb. And you remember how the father gloried in the good news when the one who had vanished suddenly appeared alive and safe!

You did not choose to go away. When a mysterious illness crept over your body, you were at the edge of lost. We were all afraid. Now you are well. Of course we rejoice! And, unlike the story, no one rejoices more than your elder brother.

*1990. November.* You lay in a hospital. No one could help. No one knew how to help. There was little thanksgiving in the prayers of that November Thursday. Our prayers were for your life.

*1990. December.* Mark lay in a hospital. No one could do anything. There was little joy in the Advent preparation that season. Our prayers were for Mark's life.

You began to improve. Soon you were out of danger. Your body began to heal, slowly. We rejoiced and continue to give thanks. You knew that physical healing could not come for Mark. I have wondered through the years how your illness affected your life. I have worried that you would remember how close in time were your illness and Mark's accident, and I feared that your relief and joy would be tainted by the knowledge of Mark's death.

What may be hard for you to understand—I want you to try—is that when Mark died, I found myself even more thankful for your recovery than I had been before. How can you understand? I do not understand. I want for us to try. Our loss makes your life immensely important for me. It is not in spite of our grief. Strangely, it feels as if it is because of my sorrow that I am filled with joy that your life is full. I want to tell you.

My experience is not the same as that of some others. I have read of some grieving parents who grow resentful when they watch other children playing gleefully or see someone else's son graduate from high school or hear the laughter of wedding celebrations—always the celebrations of others' children.

I too know of the yearning sadness of those moments. In church, I watch two lively little brothers gingerly pick Cheerios out of their dad's hand. I can see Mark and David, carefully selecting bites from their cache of "O's." My heart aches and I wipe away tears. And yet, in the same moment, joy overtakes me. I know joy and thanksgiving for the blessings of this treasured family. I understand sadness. Among my panoply of feelings, I have not found resentment.

We celebrated a wedding. I grieved that my firstborn son would never have a wedding. I mourned the empty space among us where Mark should have been.

And at the same time, what joy we felt.

I worry at times that another mother will not tell me about the scholarship her son has won or the plans for his new job. I am troubled when a friend hesitates as he begins to talk of the close call his daughter had while driving home, and his relief at her safety. I fear they will not tell me the good things that happen for their children, because they worry it will hurt me. Some do not talk of their children at all, or mine. Do they imagine I will not think about Mark if they do not mention their children? Do they think I will forget Mark's death if they do not talk of their children's lives?

I yearn to be able to talk about Mark and the good parts of his life, as well as the sadness. I yearn to hear the good news of others. It is simple to say that, having known this life-wrenching loss, I never want to see others have to go through it. And so I am thankful when others know joy and not the grief I know. But I suspect it is more than that. I want you to understand. I want to understand.

I have watched the radically different paths people can take when they experience tragedy and discover how fragile life is. One is to close down and not feel, to distrust life. Another is to decide that—because life is too short and too fragile—we will drink deeply not only of the heights and depths of our own joys and sorrows, but will also put our arms around the intensities of the lives of others, the very good and the tragic.

I know it is more complicated than that. We all close down at first, in the face of tragedy. We can do no other. We cannot take it in all at once. More than ten years later, I am still taking in the reality of Mark's death. You are still taking in the reality of your having been at the edge of lost. It will be years before we can face all that September 11th has meant for us.

But some stay closed, all closed. My life is over, they say. I will never risk anything. I will not let those I love risk. I dare not be happy again or love again. Leave me alone. Let me live my career of pain. How does it happen that something breaks through the closed-ness? How does my world, your world, open and expand?

I watch you when we are together. I watch you and your tenderness with other people. You do it all gently, quietly. You link with friends. You reach into the lives of others. Your care makes a broad sweep into the world around you.

How did your illness affect that? Do you know? Can you know? It is not only death that changes lives. Your gift of health has given to you a depth of connecting and caring even greater than you knew before.

I watch from a distance, and what I see in you is one who knows life is fragile and so will live it to its fullest and love and enjoy and risk. You will also absorb more profoundly the pain and sorrow of others, for you have known that so deeply. That is how I want to live. That is my vision of what can happen when one has known loss or been to the edge. I want to drink deeply not only of the heights and depths of my own joys and sorrows. I want to put my arms around the intensities of the lives of others.

I recall a night when many gathered at the home of friends after their son died. I do not recall any words I spoke, only touches and looks and shaking my head. While I watched, a grieving mother came to our friend, weeping uncontrollably. Her adult child had died more than twenty years before. I had watched her at other times, over many years, as she struggled to go on with her life. A career of pain. A hardness and bitterness that never left her.

I was sitting by another mother, one whose son had died several years before Mark. Her family had been for me a beacon, a sign that, no matter how awful it was, they were alive. I want to be like that: to witness for others who know loss that you can be miraculously alive, even when you do not think you will live, even when you are not sure you want to live.

Did you ever see Stuart in his clown make up? When he became BaBa, he had a ministry that was marvelous in its power. He delighted children and surprised wary adults into warm smiles. I saw new life come to BaBa and to those around him.

How does it happen that some folks stay closed, all closed, and others are blessed with the mystery of becoming alive?

I can see BaBa/Stuart handing a delicate daisy to a wide-eyed child, for sharing daisies has become a blessed part of who he is. And each time he comes home with an armful of those magical flowers, or picks a wild daisy for me as we walk through a meadow, I know anew the delight of that child. I know a gift of love and life.

It is for me a poignant, if imperfect, reflection of the One who came that we might have life, and have it in its miraculous abundance. I know life anew.

It is a gift that our worlds have opened, and opened wider than they ever were before. It is a miracle for which I have no word but "alive." And then, we drink more deeply not only of the heights and depths of our own joys and sorrow, but also spread our arms wide around the intensities of the lives of others.

I am now more alive to the pain of another's loss. In the wake of September 11th, I feel as if the air and earth and sea and sky are so full of wails and tears, I can hardly bear it. And in the same moment, I am overtaken with joy both that my David is safe and also that the daughter of another mother—one I know only from a blurred moment on the television news—is saved.

Drink deeply, my young friend, and enter into your joy and your sorrow. And keep opening your heart wide, as I have watched you do, to all that is around you, the heights and the depths, the celebrations and tragedies. I want to understand it all. I want you to understand. Neither of us will, completely. But try. Try. And believe that—finally—in the midst of all we suffer, Isaiah speaks:

So the LORD's people shall come back, set free . . .
joy and gladness shall overtake them as they come,
and sorrow and sighing shall flee away.

My prayers,

*Susan*

# To Etta Mae and Fritz

## Dear Etta Mae and Fritz,

Your book is remarkable. *Dancing in a Wheelchair*. Even the title announces that this story will not end in despair. I cried often as I read it, for I could feel your tears on many pages. What a gift you have offered to the church and to all of us who want to walk with you.

You capture poignantly the details of Tim's and Fred's lives and personalities. Although I knew them a little, and felt I knew them through you, I discovered much more from your book than "putting a face on AIDS." You showed all of us what precious children of God they were and are, what rich gifts they offered during their too-short lives, and how the world and the church have been changed because of them.

Thank you. Thank you for what you have done and are doing. Thank you for your friendship and care, for being there through these ten years and for putting words to what I could not yet say. How our lives and griefs have intertwined. I remember the day I learned of Tim's and Fred's illness. I cried for a long time. In 1989, it meant that Tim and Fred were dying.

My greatest fear had always been losing one of my boys. You were losing two. How could you go on? It was not until years later, when you sent me the draft of the lectures Fritz had presented for other bishops, that I began to understand.

> There was no way through that experience except by the way of anguished prayer. . . . That prayer life led us into a new relationship with the Scriptures and a new awareness that God was with us in this terrible time. We began to live "in Christ," know his sufferings, trust his healing, hope in his resurrection. We became more open to the leading of the Spirit. Our experience was revealing the meaning of spirituality to us.

I watched from a distance as you suffered through those months. As I read your book about your boys, I realized how little I knew about what you faced. Seeing your children with an illness so little understood, so maligned, so devastating of body and spirit—I could not imagine.

What a peculiar turning of what some call fate: Our Mark died first. It was a week before your Tim. I remember you at the visitation. You looked at me with an understanding that was palpable. We all three shook our heads. We did not need words. You understood more than I did. You knew.

There was no way through that experience except by the way of anguished prayer. As I listened and read of your experience, I found parallels with my own. When Mark died, the world changed for us, and, like you, what I knew about prayer and life in the Spirit was profoundly reshaped. It was as if a veil lifted.

The anguish and grief and despair of watching Mark die led me to a hunger to live in God's presence that I had not known was possible. Spiritual guides come in many forms, and grief and despair are not the only avenues to such craving. Nor does tragedy always lead one *toward* God's presence. I only witness, like you, to my own experience. A veil lifted, and anguish became an opening to what lay beyond.

And yet, I sometimes ask myself, Is this the only way? What of those whose lives seem privileged? Those spared from suffering? In the same vein that Paul asked, "Should we continue in sin in order that grace may abound?" are we to seek suffering that our life in the Spirit may be deepened? Surely not.

Are our words, then, only significant for those who are fellow sufferers?

It may be we are called, if only for them, to keep witnessing to the ways in which God has taken our sackcloth, torn it apart, and woven it into a shawl for prayer. And how God has taken us in our wheelchairs and taught us to dance.

That would be enough. That is what you did for me. And yet, veils lift in many ways. We know colleagues who are untouched by suffering—or we think we know. How do we know? How can we know the hidden wounds and broken dreams? How can we see into the fears unspoken, the hidden alienations, the well-disguised despair? Might our witness be for them too? Perhaps they also can come to know that nothing need be wasted, not even what is most wounding.

*Dancing in a Wheelchair.* When you gave your book that curious title, you described not only those moments of joy your boys knew in the midst of devastating illness. You also, of course, described yourselves. The power of your witness is that you do not pretend that you have to get out of the wheelchair to dance. The power of your word to me is that I will always carry with me the wounds of loss, and with them—no, because of them—I am able to dance beyond a veil I did not know was there.

Dance on, my dear friends. Dance on.

Fondly,

*Susan*

# To My Dear Ones

## My Dearest Friends,

You have saved my life. You, who have been there rightly, saved my life.

You are legion. It requires a legion to save the life of a grieving mother. My grieving is too much for one of you. Together, you saved my life.

At first, many were there. Some went away. I frightened them. The books say isolation surrounds grieving parents. I did not understand why some went away. Now I have begun to see. If one of us can lose a child, who else can? Did I remind them it could happen to them? They did not know what to say.

You stayed. You may have been frightened, but you stayed. Some went away. I worried them. I did not get better. Some days I was worse. They did not know what to do with me.

I did not get better, but you stayed. You did not always know what to do. You knew how to be here, beside me, without doing anything. Some went away. I irritated them. I wanted to talk about Mark. They got tired of listening. Get on with your life, they said. No, they did not *say* it, but they meant it.

You asked about Mark. You asked about me and about Mark. You wanted to hear. You let me talk. You asked me to talk. You knew that was how I was getting on with my life. You are legion, but, in truth, you are a precious few, precious and treasured. I know you by the tone of your voice, the way you ask how I am. I recognize the look, the look that *knows*. I feel the touch—an embrace that lasts a moment longer than it needs to.

You do not forget. You listen, and you do not forget. You see tears, and you do not ask what happened. You know it is about Mark and me. You simply say, "Tell me." Ten years later, you know there are moments. Some moments last a season. Other moments, but a moment.

You differ from one another:

You are not a parent. How could you know? At the beginning, you looked across the table, and your face bore the pain I could not yet feel. You wrote, and wrote again, and again. You put words to the anguish that was forming around my heart. How could you know?

You raised bright and healthy boys, like Mark and David. Ten years ago, tragedy and illness had not yet swept over your family. But you already knew. Your eyes searched for how I was going on.

Your children have challenged you. Hard times. Sad times. They have grown up now. They have all grown up. They are alive and safe and creating good futures. How can you understand?

You are childless. Once you were not, and now you are. I know you understand. That is not a mystery. The mystery, the miracle, is that you can step from your pain and into mine.

You have saved my life.

You have been there rightly, and you are saving my life. At the beginning, you sat by me. You stayed. You, who must always be *doing*, sat with me. Jewish tradition has a name for it: "sitting shivah." For seven days, mourners sit shivah. Motionlessness. A time to sit with grief and remembering and weeping. It is not a time to sit alone.

You cleaned my house and brought food I did not believe I wanted. I found comfort in your food. You sat with me. You cried when I was afraid to start. You love Mark. You love me. You love David and Stuart. You came to tell us.

You have saved my life.

In the beginning, you stayed with me. You stayed by me. I was not sure I could go on. You thought I could. I did, for one more day, and then one more. One more week. One more month. A year. You should be better now, some said. It has been a year. You said nothing about better. You stayed close by. You asked. You listened. You asked me to do what I did not believe I could do. You stayed close by while I tried. You kept asking. I kept trying. One more month. Another year.

I remembered a poem and could not find it. You found it. You understood it was important when I could not explain why.

You asked me to speak at a funeral. I was not sure I could. You said I did it well. I believed you. You asked me, again, to do what I did not believe I could do. You stayed close by, again, while I tried. You kept asking. I began to believe I could. You said I was doing well. One day I made a mistake. I knew it was not a little mistake, and you did too. You asked me what I learned. I knew then you believed I could keep going. Another year.

All the timetables said I should be much better. I was, sometimes. But there were moments. Fewer understood. You understand. You ask and listen and do not forget.

You are saving my life.

You do not try to play psychologist. You have not read the books about bereavement and unresolved grief and illegitimate guilt and the tasks of mourning. It is a good thing. Some of the books are wrong. A few are not wrong. A few help me know I am not crazy. You help me know too.

From one I have discovered new words for my grieving. I tell them to you because I think you already know. You have known, without having the words.

When Mark died, I lost part of me. Unlike an ordinary wound, it is more like dismemberment, losing my right arm. It requires learning to live with my irretrievable loss. Healing does not restore. Rather I have to learn a gradual acceptance of pain, pain that fluctuates in intensity and "changes in complexion." But it may not diminish and never goes away.

One bereft mother read that description and nodded knowingly. Then she added, "If you lose an arm, everyone can see it. They see that you have to live the rest of your life without your arm. But our loss is invisible." Yes, our loss becomes invisible as the months and years go by. It is invisible—unless you look, and listen, very carefully.

You already know that. You heard me read the words from that book and said I should write them in huge letters on a gigantic poster so everyone could see them: THE PAIN NEVER GOES AWAY. You understand. You are one of the precious, treasured few. You have stayed with me, sat shivah for ten years with me. You knew I had to learn to live with my loss, to reshape my life around my pain. You saw that it did not go away. You saw that it would not go away, and still I was going on with my life. You saw I had to learn, and I could not sit alone.

You saved my life.

How did you know how? How did you learn? What did you know that others did not? You know how to love. You know the kind of love that steps into another's pain. You know how to love rightly.

I have long been wary of how some interpret "Love your neighbor as yourself," that you should treat me as you want to be treated. But I am not you. How can you know how to love me if you are the measure of that love? I choose rather the wisdom of the Hasidic story: A rabbi repeatedly counters his student's "I love you" with "Do you know what hurts me?" and finally explains, "How can you love me if you do not know what hurts me?"

You know how to love. You know love that steps into my pain. You listen and learn. And so you understand. You stay and sit. You invite and challenge. When you see enough strength, you chastise and correct; and strength increases. You love. You love enough to stay and sit and listen until you *know*. And then you know how to love rightly.

You have saved my life.

I know Mark is dead. My loss is forever. The pain will never disappear. Because you have stepped into my pain with me, I am going on with my life. You know how to love. You do not go away.

Thank you for saving my life.

*Susan*

# To Mark

## Mark, My Dear Mark,

Now you are safe. You are cradled in God's love, and God now will wipe away your tears and keep you safe. I picture you gathered up and cared for by Creta and Grandmother and Granddaddy Lee, who all loved you so, and by Mom and Pop Sonnenday, who never knew you here. Strange how I have—and need—physical images of your being loved and cradled in death, when I used to be surprised that others had them.

For so long I worried about you. I know it troubled you. I worried about your not finding a calling, or even a job, that you found challenging, that you could love. You had such hopes, such dreams. The end of the rainbow was in the next opportunity—a job with Lee and Cathy in Florida, a new company starting in California, the football and baseball board games you worked to perfect. Did you enjoy your "now"? How can I find words for how extraordinary you were? Extra-ordinary. Extra-curious. Extra-bright. Extra-tender in your care.

How skilled you were as you taught and explained those

complexities you could understand so clearly. When you were explaining to me an economic theory you were studying, you drew diagrams and taught me meticulously, patiently. Your mind wrapped around knowledge I could not grasp. You began to teach me about computers. Recently I had to admit that I resisted moving very far into the computer world because I know how well you could have taught me—and I do not want to learn from anyone else. (I will, though. I will not like it, but I will.)

What a marvelous capacity you had for being a friend. I wish you could read the letters from those who miss you so. I pray that they told you while you were alive. Your cadre of Tufts friends write of the void "only Mark could fill." Two drove all night to be here for your service. They speak of your knack for making someone feel special, your fierce loyalty, your good heart. You had so much love to give. You were accepting of their ordinariness, their bad times. Mark, did you know how they felt? Could you believe it?

I wanted you to be happy, and I feared too often you were not happy. I wanted you to know how much others cared for you and regarded you, but I fear you did not believe how wide and deep that care spread. I wanted you to be assured that my expectations were not for you to do some "successful" thing, measured by others' standards. I wanted you to do what would be engaging and satisfying for you, and I fear you were not assured very often.

I wanted you to know how completely I loved you—and love you still—and I shall always cherish the conviction that you did—and do—know that. The last time you were home, you and I were up before dawn so you could get an early start. We sat at the old oak table, and it squeaked a bit as we leaned our elbows on it, drank our coffee, talked of your trip. It was the table where we had been together for twenty-three years. Such memories it holds. On your first birthday, you had to stretch out of your high chair to blow out your candle, and then curiously shaped cakes held more and more candles as years went on. The carefully designed place mats you and David made soon were spotted with spaghetti sauce, but that made them more precious to me. Then your own culinary creations found their way to that table: omelets with *very* unusual ingredients, moussaka from scratch, and your unique variations on the familiar box of macaroni and cheese.

It was our game table too. I thought "Sorry!" was a children's game of chance, but soon you could see strategies and devise splendid tactics. I thought Monopoly was for recreation; for you, it was a study in business management. And, as your friends often said, you should have auditioned for a game show. When Trivial Pursuit was set up at that table, I listened with awe, and not a little envy, as you drew from resources I could not imagine you had.

What fun we could have. How intriguing it was to watch your mind work. I miss your mind. I miss your strategies and tactics and memory and imagination. I miss you so much.

We sat at the table for the last time. You drank your coffee. The last time. What if we had known? What would we have said? I sometimes still sit at that table and wonder. I no longer put four chairs around the table, only three. I look at the empty place and wonder.

I poured you a cup of coffee to take with you. We stood for a moment on the back steps. I stood on my tiptoes and hugged you hard. "I love you," I whispered. I treasure the way you answered when you were little: "I know that, Mommy." That morning you smiled. "I love you, too, Mom."

It was still dark. You got into the car and put on the seat belt. I said, characteristically, "Please, please, be careful," and you backed slowly, carefully, out of the driveway. I watched until I could see you no longer. I was frightened. You were driving alone, all the way to California. Each time you called from the road, I felt a little more confident. You were safe, and you did not have much farther to go. I also felt glad that you were reveling in the beauty of what you were seeing.

You made it safely. I worried less about you. Your work would start soon. You found odd jobs for the in-between time. As ever, you found friends, and delighted in their children. You invented bedtime stories and taught shoe-tying.

December came. The afternoon when you called, we were on our way out the door, and I asked if I could call you back later. How I wish I would have stopped and talked, and listened. Would it have made any difference? Thank heaven, I will never know. But thank heaven I said to you, as always, "I love you." And you said, "I love you, too, Mom."

As your dad and Tracy and I stood keeping vigil at your bedside, we said, over and over, "We love you, Mark." And we could each rest in the assurance that you knew that. We had heard you say that you knew it. You died knowing how much you were loved.

One nurse who cared for you showed us how a reading on an intricate machine measured increased response from you as we talked. (You would have been intrigued by it.) She suggested we leave or be quiet when you grew agitated. We knew that you were very far from us by that time. We will not ever know what you heard and if you understood anything. We believe that you knew we were there, and in your days of dying, as in every day of living, you knew you were not alone. You knew you were surrounded by love.

Many have said to me since you died, "I think that must be the worst thing that can happen—to lose a child." As I think of what else might have happened on that highway early on Sunday morning, I think of what *you* would have found "worse." A kind woman called and then wrote to us.

You had passed them on the highway—not going too fast, she said—and had nodded and smiled at them. Right over the hill you saw cars backed up, and to avoid them, you had to brake quickly. The car rolled over. No other cars were touched. No one else was hurt.

I imagine how it would have been for you had you been all right, and someone else critically injured or killed. What if you had had a friend with you, or the child you had taught to tie her shoes, and you had then stood by a bed as we did by yours? How would it have been for you, for all of us, to go on living when others were lost? I remember the paralyzing guilt and hurt you felt when you thought you had caused others pain. How would you have faced this kind of death? We would have tried to be with you. We would have found ways, but I fear there would have been no end to your suffering. Is your death the very worst thing that could have happened for you, for us all?

Or what if you had survived? We knew there had been such damage to your brain, to your extraordinary mind. We hoped for a miracle. Had you survived, we would have continued to hope for miracle upon miracle. I think we already felt in our hearts that the "you" we had known and loved was already lost to us. We kept hoping and hoping—and grieving.

What if you had survived? Grandmother's good friend Sister Luke wrote to send her love to us when she learned you had died. She told us of her friend whose son had been critically injured and had survived with severe brain damage. Her friend told Sister Luke, "I have always loved Richard; and now I will learn to love a different Richard." We have always loved you, and we would surely have learned to love a different Mark. Just as we grieve your death now, we would have grieved the death of the you that we knew, and learned to love again.

My friend Michael returned to campus with word that his thirty-year-old son and his son's family had been in an accident. Michael's daughter-in-law died, his grandchild was not seriously hurt, and his son had traumatic head injuries. Michael said that as he and his wife went to the hospital that night, it was hard to know what to pray for. Their son did live, and now they care for their son and their grandchild as two children. They rejoice in the small steps that each one takes and the new words that each speaks.

Michael and I have cried together and pray for each other. We have said, and thought, Which is harder? Which would we choose? And give thanks that we did not have to choose. The worst thing that can happen. Who can know? At the end of his story about the death of his daughter and her family, William Wharton writes of his wife and himself: "I know we've independently decided the same thing. The worst has happened. The only thing worse would be to let it ruin our lives, our children's, our friends'."

The worst. And yet there can be worse. I do not know what is worst. I know I miss you terribly. I ache each day. Our lives have changed forever.

I know you are safe in God's love. I constantly give thanks for your life and for all you gave to me and taught me, in your living and in your dying. I dare not make it worse. I will live. I will remember and cherish the good memories. I will craft a forgiven past into an asset for a dedicated future. I will live what you gave to me and taught me. I will know joy in the morning. I promise.

Mark, my dearest Mark. I love you. But then, you know that.

*Mom*

# Afterword: Recomposing My Life

As the years have passed, I have grown dissatisfied with the notion of grief as a "life transition." It sounds placid, natural. What could be more unnatural, more wrenching, than burying your child? And then trying to live a life without the one you treasured?

I had an intimation at the beginning: Life would never be the same. Mark was dead. He would never, ever, be a part of our lives in the way he had been. We had to figure out life without him.

Everything was torn to pieces. I wondered if any pieces would fit together again—ever. I had to reassemble my life, and beloved pieces would always be missing. I had to recompose my life, with misshapen pieces that I had always dreaded.

I looked ahead and worried that my life would always be agony and tears, with pain as the defining emotion of each day. But slowly, ever so slowly, I am composing a new kind of normal. I am discovering ways to reassemble my life without Mark *and* with the Mark I will forever love.

At first, I tried to keep doing the same things, but they were not the same. Everything was strange—for all of us.

Tracy, Mark's stepmother, said she tried to go Christmas shopping in the days after the memorial service. All she could see were gifts for Mark. She kept returning home.

Stuart offered to do the grocery shopping. No. I needed to go, too, as we always did. When we got there, the first thing I saw was an endearing blond three-year-old who looked like Mark when he was little. I wanted to go to his mother and say, "Delight in him! Treasure him. Be thankful for him each moment." We tried to live "normally," and everywhere we turned, the world was no longer the same. What is it to live into a new kind of normal? After five years, I began to glimpse how.

I recalled a passage from *Ordinary People*. Strange that it stayed with me, when I refused even to fear that such a loss would touch our lives. The surviving brother leans against the window of a travel agency, looking at the poster that reminds him of their family's glorious skiing trips together. He awaits the familiar "arrow of pain." "Only there is none. An oddly pleasant swell of memory, a wave of warmth flooding over him, sliding back, slowly. It is a first."

It comes. Sometimes. Each joy is touched with a wish that Mark could be here too. When the Chiefs play at their best, there is joy mixed with such longing. How Mark would have *loved* this. And then comes a moment like C. S. Lewis described:

> Tonight all the hells of young grief have opened up again; the mad words, the bitter resentment, the fluttering in the stomach, the nightmare unreality, the wallowed-in tears. For in grief nothing "stays put." One keeps on emerging from a phase, but it always recurs. Round and round. Everything repeats. Am I going in circles, or dare I hope I am on a spiral?

Dare I hope?

Years ago, in another life it seems, I was part of an interpretive dance group and danced "Joy and Sorrow" from Kahlil

Gibran's *The Prophet*. Although what I once thought was pro-found in Gibran now seems less so, there remains one line whose truth I am coming to know: "The deeper that sorrow carves within your being, the more joy you can contain."

I could not have understood it then, anymore than I knew what the psalmist meant. "Those who go out weep-ing, bearing the seed for sowing, shall come home with shouts of joy, carrying their sheaves." I could not have understood it in those early days and weeks and months. All I knew was weeping and sorrow. Then it was as if a mist lifted, and I found more weeping and sorrow. Yet, with less mist, I could begin to have a glimpse of how joy might look, and feel. One mother spoke of hearing some-one laugh, looking around, and discovering, to her sur-prise, that it was *she* who was laughing.

Later, I found there was sorrow still hidden. As the cov-ering mist lifted, I saw that I missed Mark at times and in ways I had not known before. Sorrow carved deeper. Then, strangely, were moments more full of joy than I could have imagined. As I sat in King's College Chapel in Cambridge one winter evening, I looked at the magnificent ceiling and exquisite carvings. I watched candles flicker and illuminate the huge Rubens painting, *Adoration of the Magi*. I listened to little boys and young men sing, *Rejoice in the Lamb*. I wept tears of thanksgiving and thought of that question Emily asks in *Our Town*, "Do any human beings ever real-ize life while they live it every, every minute?"

I am alive, in a fragile, precious life. Can I realize it, every, every minute? My life will never get back to normal. And yet, in tiny, incremental ways, a new kind of normal grows. I discover and create it. I compose and assemble and wonder at it. My life has gifts in it that I would never have known had Mark lived. I have bonded in companion-ship with other parents whose wisdom and care and jour-ney I would never have known.

I am in an unsought covenant with sisters and brothers

in Christ whose lives I would have known only from afar. What a remarkable blessing. (Of course, I am also familiar with what William Sloane Coffin said after his son's death, "[What I learn] better be good, given the price.")

In grief the world can become small and isolated. But mine, in time, has become larger and larger. It *is* a blessing—the good that God has worked in the midst of agony. But the sorrow and the blessing live together. It is not so raw now. One kind of healing is happening. And yet, when I read words of Julian of Norwich, I wonder if this is the way it will always be.

> . . . I was at peace, at ease and at rest, so that there was nothing upon earth which could have afflicted me.
>
> This lasted only for a time, and then I was changed. . . . I felt that there was no ease or comfort for me except hope, faith and love, and truly I felt very little of this. And then presently God gave me again comfort and rest for my soul. . . . And then again I felt the pain, and then afterward the joy and the delight, now the one and now the other, again and again.

It helps me to know that she felt that way, and she is still called a beloved foremother in the faith. I remember she could also trust the promise she heard from her Lord: "all will be well," and "every kind of thing will be well." I am composing a new kind of normal, with a new form of wisdom, and a new measure of joy that lives beside sorrow.

> "Weeping may linger for the night,"
>    and the night is very long,
> But morning does come,
>    and with morning, the promise of joy.

*Susan*

# Notes

## Our World Changed Forever

**9** "Praise be to the God . . ." (2 Cor. 1:3-4 NEB).
**12** Margaret Atwood, *The Blind Assassin* (New York: Nan A. Talese, 2000), p. 283.
**12** Anna Quindlan, "How Dark? How Stormy? I Can't Recall?" *The New York Times Book Review*, 11 May 1997, sec. 7, p. 34, final edition.

## To My Wise Teacher

**16** Roger Kahn, *The Boys of Summer* (New York: Harper & Row, 1972), p. 30.
**16** "If we live, we live to the Lord . . ." (Rom. 14:8).
**18** H. Richard Niebuhr, quoted in Aidan Kavanagh, "Opinion: Death and Life," *Reflections* (winter–spring, 1992), pp. 27-28.
**19** Bishop Dehqani-Tafti, "A Father's Prayer Upon the Murder of His Son," in *The Oxford Book of Prayer*, ed. George Appleton (London: Oxford University Press, 1989), p. 136.

## To Our Pastor

**21** James Cleveland, "Somehow I Made It" © 1990 by James Cleveland Music BMI, Savgos Music BMI. All rights reserved. Used by permission.
**22** Joan D. Chittister, OSB, *The Psalms: Meditations for Every Day of the Year* (New York: Crossroad, 1996), pp. 44, 50.

**23** John Newton, "Amazing Grace."

**24** Gardner Taylor, "A Wide Vision Through a Narrow Window," quoted in Michael Eric Dyson, *Christian Century,* "Gardner Taylor: Poet Laureate of the Pulpit" (January 4-11, 1995), p. 16.

## *To Witnesses in Song*

**25** James Cleveland, "Somehow I Made It."

**27** Charles Nicks, "I Can Depend on God" © Copyright 1991 by Bridgeport Music Inc. (BMI). All Rights reserved. Used By Permission.

**29** "I want to bring you some spiritual gift . . . " (Rom. 1:11*b*-12 NEB).

**29** "pots of earthenware" (2 Cor. 4:7 NEB).

**31** "abundantly far more . . . " (Eph. 3:20).

## *To My Husband*

**38** Paraphrased from *The United Methodist Book of Worship* (Nashville: The United Methodist Publishing House, 1992), pp. 157, 163.

## *To My Son David*

**44** "The deeper that sorrow carves within your being . . ." Kahlil Gibran, *The Prophet* (New York: Alfred A. Knopf, 1987), p. 32.

## *To Mark's Father*

**47** "I am the product of two generations. . ." Cathy Guisewite, quoted in Henri Rix, "Hanging in There," *Kansas City Star,* 4 October 1984, p. 1B.

**48** "Boys build houses . . . " Whitney Darrow Jr., *I'm Glad I'm a Boy! I'm Glad I'm a Girl!* (New York: Windmill Books, 1970).

## *To My Father*

**56** "Everliving God, this day revives in us memories of loved ones . . . " paraphrased from *The United Methodist Church Book of Worship* (Nashville: The United Methodist Publishing House, 1992), p. 548.

## *To My Mother*

**61** Adrienne Rich, *Of Woman Born: Motherhood As Experience and Institution* (New York: W. W. Norton & Company, 1995), p. 235.